STEP-BY-STEP
WRITING

BOOK 1

A STANDARDS-BASED APPROACH

Linda Lonon Blanton

HEINLE
CENGAGE Learning

Australia • Brazil • Japan • Korea • Mexico • Singapore • Spain • United Kingdom • United States

HEINLE
CENGAGE Learning

STEP-BY-STEP Writing, Book 1:
A Standards-Based Approach,
Second Edition
Linda Lonon Blanton

Publisher, School ESL: Phyllis Dobbins

Director of Content Development:
Anita Raducanu

Senior Development Editor: Rebecca Klevberg

Associate Editor: Emily Dendinger

Editorial Assistant: Catherine McCue

Director of Product Marketing: Amy Mabley

Executive Marketing Manager:
Jim McDonough

Senior Production Editor: Maryellen E. Killeen

Senior Frontlist Buyer: Marcia Locke

Project Management and Composition:
Pre-PressPMG

Cover Design: Sibler Design

For product information and technology assistance, contact us at
Cengage Learning Customer & Sales Support, 1-800-354-9706
For permission to use material from this text or product,
submit all requests online at **cengage.com/permissions**
Further permissions questions can be emailed to
permissionrequest@cengage.com

ISBN 10: 1-4240-0400-4
ISBN 13: 978-1-4240-0400-3

ISE ISBN 10: 1-4240-0503-5
ISE ISBN 13: 978-1-4240-0503-1

Heinle
25 Thomson Place
Boston, MA 02210
USA

Cengage Learning is a leading provider of customized learning solutions with office locations around the globe, including Singapore, the United Kingdom, Australia, Mexico, Brazil, and Japan. Locate our local office at:
international.cengage.com/region

Cengage Learning products are represented in Canada by Nelson Education, Ltd.

Visit Heinle online at **elt.heinle.com**

Visit our corporate website at **cengage.com**

Printed in Canada
4 5 6 7 8 9 10 11

ACKNOWLEDGMENTS

Heinle would like to thank the following consultants and reviewers:

Consultants

Jennifer Runner
Atwater High School
Atwater, California

Patricia Levine
Colts Neck High School
Colts Neck, New Jersey

Alicia Bartol-Thomas
Sarasota County Schools
Sarasota, Florida

Vivian K. Kahn
Halsey Intermediate School 296
New York City Dept. of Education
Brooklyn, New York

Reviewers

Teresa Arvizu
McFarland Unified School District
McFarland, California

M. Danielle Bragaw
Bedichek Middle School
Austin, Texas

Gary Bechtold
New Boston Pilot Middle School
Dorchester, Massachusetts

Maria Celis
Lamar High School
Houston, Texas

Linda Contreras
Luther Burbank High School
Sacramento, California

Susannah Courand
T.C. Williams High School
Alexandria, Virginia

Dana Dusbiber
Luther Burbank High School
Sacramento, California

Sara Farley
Wichita High School East
Wichita, Kansas

Sharolyn Hutton
Newcomer School
Ontario, California

Barbara Ishida
Downey High School
Modesto, California

Dana Liebowitz
Palm Beach Central High School
Wellington, Florida

Barbara M. Linde
YorkTown, Virginia

Andrew Lukov
School District of Philadelphia
Philadelphia, Pennsylvania

Jennifer Olsen
Chiefess Kamakahelei Middle
    School
Lihue, Hawaii

Mary Susan Osborn-Iratene
Will Rogers Middle School
Fair Oaks, California

Diana Sefchik
North Plainfield High School
North Plainfield, New Jersey

Malgorzata Stone
Franklin High School
Seattle, Washington

Alison Tepper
Western Middle School
Greenwich, Connecticut

Mark Trzasko
Okeeheelee Middle School
West Palm Beach, Florida

Karin VonRiman
Abraham Clark High School
Roselle, New Jersey

Deborah Wilkes
Lee County High School
Sanford, North Carolina

Clara Wolfe
William Allen High School
Allentown, Pennsylvania

TABLE OF CONTENTS

TO THE STUDENT

How to use this book

Discuss
Talk about the pictures.

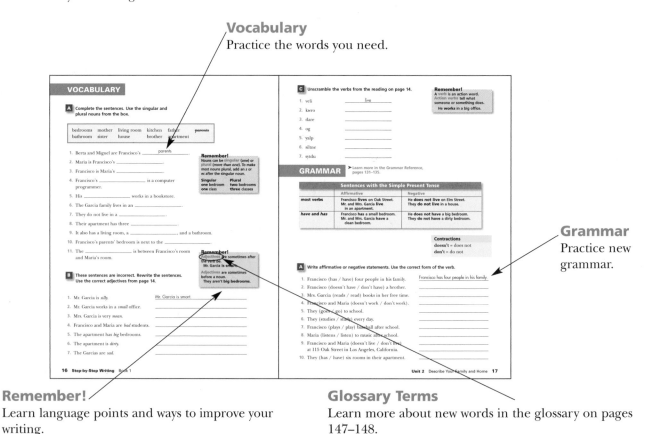

Read
Read a short passage. This models new language you can use for your writing.

Write Captions
Write captions to describe the pictures. This helps to understand how to use new words and sentences.

Vocabulary
Practice the words you need.

Grammar
Practice new grammar.

Remember!
Learn language points and ways to improve your writing.

Glossary Terms
Learn more about new words in the glossary on pages 147–148.

Organization
Practice ways to organize information.

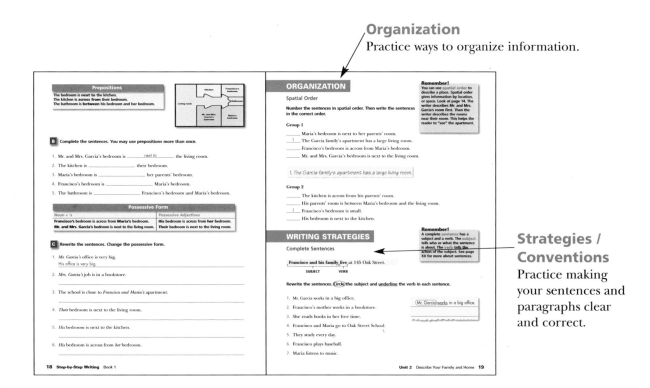

Strategies / Conventions
Practice making your sentences and paragraphs clear and correct.

Writing
See a model of a student's writing. This helps you understand your goal.

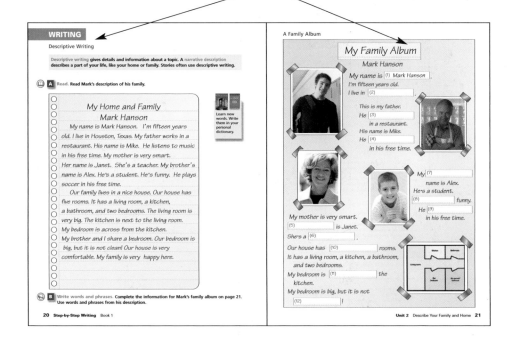

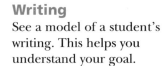

(continued on the following page)

Writing Prompt
Read the writing prompt. This tells you what to do.

Step 1: Pre-write
Look at model notes and a graphic organizer. Then you think of ideas and take notes.

Step 3: Draft and Revise
Look at a model first draft and make corrections. Then you write your own first draft. You think of how to improve your writing. Then you revise your writing.

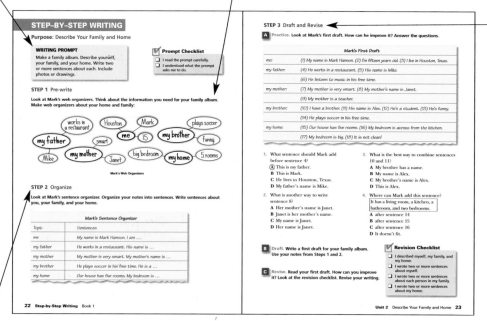

Step 2: Organize
You put your ideas in order. This will help the reader to understand your writing.

Step 4: Edit
Find errors in model sentences and correct them. Then, you edit your own draft. In Peer Edit, exchange drafts with a partner. Then make suggestions for improvement.

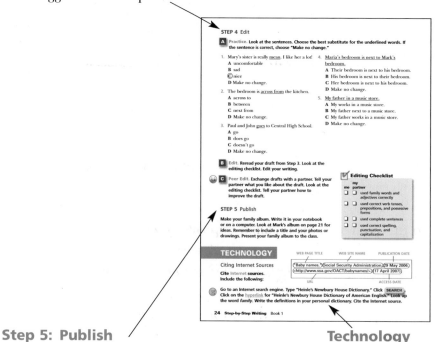

Step 5: Publish
Make a final draft of your writing. Now you can share it with your class or your family.

Technology
Use a computer to find and format new information.

Why is writing important?

With good writing skills, you can:

 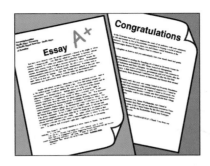 

Connect	Succeed	Express
- connect with people	- do better in school	- describe and explain your experiences
	- get a job or get into college	
- write letters, e-mail, instructions, speeches, posters, articles, descriptions, and summaries	- write essays, book reports, applications, and persuasive business letters	- write journal entries, descriptions, stories, and poems

What are good writing habits?

Good writers think about . . .	Questions	Examples
Form	What does the writing look like?	a letter, a paragraph, a list
Audience	Who will read my writing?	a friend, a teacher, someone I don't know
Topic	What is the writing about?	my weekend, my school, a celebration
Purpose	Why am I writing?	to describe, to inform, to persuade

What are the types of writing?

Are you writing to describe someone? Are you writing to tell how something looks, tastes, feels, smells, sounds? This is called **descriptive writing.**

Are you writing to tell about something that happened? This is called **narrative writing.**

Are you writing to explain facts to the reader? This is called **expository writing.**

Do you want the reader to do something? This is called **persuasive writing.**

Are you writing to explain a process or procedure? This is called **technical writing.**

Are you writing a message to someone? This is called **letter writing.**

Are you writing about something you read? This is called a **response to literature.**

Unit 1

Give Information about Yourself

UNIT OBJECTIVES

Writing
informational writing

Organization
categorize by topic

Writing Conventions
capitalization

Vocabulary
classroom words with articles
adjectives
numbers 1 to 20

Grammar
statements with *be*
subject pronouns

Technology
searching the Internet with
keywords

CENTRAL SCHOOL
STUDENT ID

Francisco Garcia
signature

Name: Francisco Garcia
Age: 15 years old

An Informational Survey

Informational Survey

Shi-Mei

First Name: (1)

Last Name: (2)

Nickname: (3)

Age: (4)

City/State: (5)

English Teacher: (6)

Teacher Description: (7)

School Name: (8)

School Address: (9)

School Description: (10)

READING

A **Discuss.** Find these people, places, and things on page 3.
Write the words under the correct topic.

desk	teacher	building	classroom
board	student	English class	

People	Places	Things
TEACHER	BUILDING	ENGLISH CLASS
STUDENT	CLASSROOM	BOARD
		DESK

B **Read.** Read the information.

Francisco's School

Francisco Garcia is a student. He is fifteen years old.
He is from Los Angeles, California. Mrs. Moore is his
English teacher. Mrs. Moore is a good teacher. She is
kind and friendly. Francisco and Mrs. Moore are in the
classroom now. They are in an English class. They are
busy. Francisco is at a desk. Mrs. Moore is not at a desk.
She is at the board. The classroom is not a big room. It
is a small room. It is clean and colorful. The classroom
is in a large building.

Learn new
words. Write
them in your
personal
dictionary.

C **Write captions.** Write a sentence for each picture on page 3.
Use sentences from the reading.

CENTRAL SCHOOL
STUDENT ID

Francisco Garcia
signature

Name: Francisco Garcia
Age: 15 years old

1. He is 15 years old.

2. _____ is from _____ California

3. Mrs. Moore is his English teacher

4. They are in the classroom now

5. Francisco is at a desk

6. She is at the board.

7. The classroom is in a huge building

VOCABULARY

A Circle the articles in the sentences. Then complete the sentences with words from the box. Use information from the reading on page 2.

desk	teacher	building	classroom
English class	student	board	

1. Francisco is (a) _____ student _____ .

2. Mrs. Moore is a __ TEACHER __ .

3. Francisco and Mrs. Moore are in an _____ ENGLISH CLASS _____ .

4. Francisco and Mrs. Moore are in the __ CLASSROOM __ now.

5. Mrs. Moore is at the __ BOARD __ .

6. Francisco is at a __ DESK __ .

7. The classroom is in a large __ BUILDING __ .

B Complete the sentences with the correct adjectives. Use information from the reading on page 2.

good	busy	large	friendly
kind	colorful	small	clean

1. Mrs. Moore is a _____ good _____ teacher.

2. Mrs. Moore is __ KIND __ and __ FRIENDLY __ .

3. Francisco and Mrs. Moore are __ BUSY __ .

4. The classroom is a __ SMALL __ room.

5. The classroom is __ CLEAN __ and __ COLORFUL __ .

6. The classroom is in a __ LARGE __ building.

C Write the correct word for each number.

eight	five	nineteen	six	three
eighteen	four	one	sixteen	twelve
eleven	fourteen	seven	ten	twenty
fifteen	nine	seventeen	thirteen	two

1. _____one_____   6. ___six___   11. ___eleven___   16. ___sixteen___

2. ___two___   7. ___seven___   12. ___twelve___   17. ___seventeen___

3. ___three___   8. ___eight___   13. ___thirteen___   18. ___eighteen___

4. ___four___   9. ___nine___   14. ___fourteen___   19. ___nineteen___

5. ___five___   10. ___ten___   15. ___fifteen___   20. ___twenty___

GRAMMAR

➤ Learn more in the Grammar Reference, pages 131–141.

Statements with *be*

Affirmative

Francisco **is** a student.
Francisco and Mrs. Moore **are** in English class.

Negative

Mrs. Moore **is not** a student.
Francisco and Mrs. Moore **are not** in Spanish class.

Contractions

isn't = is not
aren't = are not

A Write *is* or *are* to complete the paragraph.

Francisco Garcia (1) __is__ a student. He (2) _____ fifteen years old. He (3) _____ from Los Angeles, California. Mrs. Moore (4) _____ his English teacher. Mrs. Moore (5) _____ a good teacher. She (6) _____ kind and friendly. Francisco and Mrs. Moore (7) _____ in the classroom now. They (8) _____ in an English class. They (9) _____ busy. Francisco (10) _____ at a desk. Mrs. Moore (11) _____ not at a desk. She (12) _____ at the board. The classroom (13) _____ not a big room. It (14) _____ a small room. It (15) _____ clean and colorful. The classroom (16) _____ in a large building.

Subject Pronouns

Name / Noun	Subject Pronoun
Francisco is a student.	**He** is a student.
Mrs. Moore is a teacher.	**She** is a teacher.
Francisco and **Mrs. Moore** are busy.	**They** are busy.
The building is large.	**It** is large.

Contractions

he's = he is   **they're** = they are
she's = she is   **it's** = it is

B The sentences below are incorrect. Write correct negative and affirmative sentences. Use a contraction and a subject pronoun in the second sentence.

1. Francisco is a teacher.

   Francisco is not a teacher. He's a student.

2. Francisco is nineteen years old.

   _Francisco isn't nineteen years old. He is _____

3. Mrs. Moore is a bad teacher.

   _Mrs. Moore is _____

4. Francisco and Mrs. Moore are in a Spanish class.

   _____ They are in A

5. Francisco is at the board.

   Francisco is not at the board. He at the desk

6. Mrs. Moore is at a desk.

   Mrs. Moore isn't at the desk. She is by the board

7. The classroom is a big room.

   _The classroom isn't a big room. The classroom is a
   small room_

8. Francisco and Mrs. Moore are in a small building.

   _Francisco and Mrs Moore aren't in a small building
   They're in a big building._

C Write the correct word for each number.

eight	five	nineteen	six	three
eighteen	four	one	sixteen	twelve
eleven	fourteen	seven	ten	twenty
fifteen	nine	seventeen	thirteen	two

1. _____one_____   6. _____six_____   11. _____eleven_____   16. _____sixteen_____
2. _____two_____   7. _____seven_____   12. _____twelve_____   17. _____seventeen_____
3. _____three_____   8. _____eight_____   13. _____thirteen_____   18. _____eighteen_____
4. _____four_____   9. _____nine_____   14. _____fourteen_____   19. _____nineteen_____
5. _____five_____   10. _____ten_____   15. _____fifteen_____   20. _____twenty_____

GRAMMAR

➤ Learn more in the Grammar Reference, pages 131–141.

Statements with *be*

Affirmative	Negative
Francisco **is** a student.	Mrs. Moore **is not** a student.
Francisco and Mrs. Moore **are** in English class.	Francisco and Mrs. Moore **are not** in Spanish class.

Contractions
isn't = is not
aren't = are not

A Write *is* or *are* to complete the paragraph.

Francisco Garcia (1) __is__ a student. He (2) _____ fifteen years old. He (3) _____ from Los Angeles, California. Mrs. Moore (4) _____ his English teacher. Mrs. Moore (5) _____ a good teacher. She (6) _____ kind and friendly. Francisco and Mrs. Moore (7) _____ in the classroom now. They (8) _____ in an English class. They (9) _____ busy. Francisco (10) _____ at a desk. Mrs. Moore (11) _____ not at a desk. She (12) _____ at the board. The classroom (13) _____ not a big room. It (14) _____ a small room. It (15) _____ clean and colorful. The classroom (16) _____ in a large building.

Subject Pronouns

Name / Noun	Subject Pronoun
Francisco is a student.	**He** is a student.
Mrs. Moore is a teacher.	**She** is a teacher.
Francisco and **Mrs. Moore** are busy.	**They** are busy.
The building is large.	**It** is large.

Contractions

he's = he is	**they're** = they are
she's = she is	**it's** = it is

B The sentences below are incorrect. Write correct negative and affirmative sentences. Use a contraction and a subject pronoun in the second sentence.

1. Francisco is a teacher.

   Francisco is not a teacher. He's a student.

2. Francisco is nineteen years old.

   Francisco isn't nineteen years old. He is _____

3. Mrs. Moore is a bad teacher.

   Mrs. Moore is not _____

4. Francisco and Mrs. Moore are in a Spanish class.

   Francisco and Mrs. _____ . They are in a English class.

5. Francisco is at the board.

   Francisco is not at the board. He _____ at the desk

6. Mrs. Moore is at a desk.

   Mrs. Moore isn't at the desk. She's at the board

7. The classroom is a big room.

   The classroom is not a big room. The classroom is a small room

8. Francisco and Mrs. Moore are in a small building.

   Francisco and Mrs. Moore aren't in a small building. They're in a big building.

ORGANIZATION

Categorize by Topic

Look at the reading on page 2. Write two more sentences about each topic in the chart.

Remember!
You can categorize information into topics. Look at page 2. Some information is about Francisco. Some information is about Mrs. Moore. Some information is about the classroom.

Francisco	Mrs. Moore	Classroom
Francisco Garcia is a student.	Mrs. Moore is an English teacher.	The classroom is not a big room.
FRANCISCO IS FIFTEEN YEARS	MRS. MOORE IS A GOOD TEACHER	THE CLASSROOM IS A SMALL ROOM
FRANCISO IS FROM LA, CALIFORNISCO.	MRS. MOORE IS AT THE BOARD.	THE CLASSROOM IS CLEAN

WRITING CONVENTIONS

Capitalization

Rewrite the information. Capitalize the correct words.

francisco's school

francisco garcia is a student. he is fifteen years old. he is from los angeles, california. mrs. moore is his english teacher. mrs. moore is a good teacher. she is kind and friendly. francisco and mrs. moore are in the classroom now. they are in an english class. they are busy. francisco is at a desk. mrs. moore is not at a desk. she is at the board. the classroom is not a big room. it is a small room. it is clean and colorful. the classroom is in a large building.

Remember!
Always capitalize:
- the first word of every sentence
  He is fifteen years old.
- names of people and places
  Mrs. Moore is from **California.**
- languages
  They are in **English** class.
- important words in titles
  The title of this book is *Step-by-Step Writing.*

Francisco Garcia is a student. He is . . .

WRITING

Informational Writing

Informational writing gives information about a topic. Information forms, surveys, and reports are examples of informational writing.

 A **Read.** Read the journal entry.

> ### My School
>
> Shi-Mei Wei
>
> My first name is Shi-Mei. My last name is Wei. My nickname is May. I am sixteen years old. I am from Brooklyn, New York. I am a student at Everton High School. My English teacher is Mr. Alvarez. He is kind and funny. My school's address is 161 North Avenue, Brooklyn, New York, 11222. My school is big and clean. It is colorful, too. My school is great!

Learn new words. Write them in your personal dictionary.

 B **Write words.** Copy the form on page 9 or make one on a computer. Complete the information for Shi-Mei's informational survey. Use words from her journal entry.

An Informational Survey

Informational Survey

First Name: (1) _____ Shi-Mei _____

Last Name: (2) _____ Wei _____

Nickname: (3) _____ MAY _____

Age: (4) _____ 16 (SIXTEEN YEARS OLD) _____

City/State: (5) _____ BROOKLYN, NEW YORK. _____

English Teacher: (6) _____ MR. ALVARES _____

Teacher Description: (7) _____ KIND AND FUNNY _____

School Name: (8) _____ EVERTON HIGH SCHOOL _____

School Address: (9) _____ 161 NORTH AV. BROOKLYN NY 11222 _____

_____

School Description: (10) _____ BIG, CLEAN, COLORFUL AND GREAT. _____

STEP-BY-STEP WRITING

Purpose: Give Information about Yourself

WRITING PROMPT

Fill out your own informational survey. Give information about yourself, your English teacher, and your school. Describe your English teacher and your school.

STEP 1 Pre-write

Look at Shi-Mei's information notes. Think about the information you need for your informational survey. Write notes for your survey.

Shi-Mei's Information Notes
Name: Shi-Mei Wei
Nickname: May
English Teacher: Mr. Alvarez
Description: kind? funny?
School Address: Brooklyn. (What street?)
School Description: ???

STEP 2 Organize

Look at Shi-Mei's information organizer. Categorize your notes into topics. Copy the chart or make one on a computer. Complete the organizer with information about you, your teacher, and your school.

Shi-Mei's Information Organizer		
me	my teacher	my school
Shi-Mei Wei	Mr. Alvarez	Everton
16	kind and ...	161 North Avenue
Brooklyn, ...		big and ...

STEP 3 Draft and Revise

A **Practice. Look at Shi-Mei's first draft. How can she improve it? Answer the questions.**

Shi-Mei's First Draft	
Informational Survey	
First Name:	(1) Shi-Mei Wei
Last Name:	(2) ?
Nickname:	(3) May
Age:	(4) 16
City/State:	(5) New York
English Teacher:	(6) Mr. Alvarez
Teacher Description:	(7) big and clean
School Name:	(8) Everton High School
School Address:	(9) 166 North Avenue, Brooklyn, New York 11222
School Description:	(10) kind and funny

1. What information in answer 1 should Shi-Mei move to answer 2?
   A Shi-Mei
   B Mei
   Ⓒ Wei
   D May

2. What information is missing in answer 5?
   A Wei,
   B Everton,
   C School,
   D Brooklyn,

3. What two answers should Shi-Mei exchange?
   A 7 and 10
   B 8 and 9
   C 8 and 10
   D 9 and 10

4. What information in answer 9 is incorrect?
   A 166
   B North Avenue
   C Brooklyn
   D New York

B **Draft. Write a first draft for your informational survey. Use your notes from Steps 1 and 2.**

C **Revise. Read your first draft. How can you improve it? Look at the revision checklist. Revise your writing.**

Revision Checklist

- ❑ My information is correct.
- ❑ My information is in the correct place.
- ❑ I included information about me, my teacher, and my school.
- ❑ I described my teacher and my school.

STEP 4 Edit

A **Practice.** Look at the sentences. Choose the best substitute for the underlined words. If the sentence is correct, choose "Make no change."

1. Mr. Jones is <u>a English teacher</u>.
   A English teacher
   B an English teacher
   C a teacher English
   D Make no change.

2. Jennifer is <u>colorful</u>.
   A student
   B kind
   C teacher
   D Make no change.

3. <u>Mrs</u>. Thomas is a good teacher. <u>He</u> is very nice.
   A It
   B She
   C His
   D Make no change.

4. <u>Pedro and Martin is</u> nice and kind.
   A Pedro and Martin are
   B Pedro and Martin is not
   C They is
   D Make no change.

5. <u>Mr. lee is from Dallas, texas.</u>
   A Mr. lee is from Dallas, Texas.
   B Mr. Lee is from Dallas, texas.
   C Mr. Lee is from Dallas, Texas.
   D Make no change.

B **Edit.** Reread your draft from Step 3. Look at the editing checklist. Edit your writing.

C **Peer Edit.** Exchange drafts with a partner. Tell your partner what you like about the draft. Look at the editing checklist. Tell your partner how to improve the draft.

STEP 5 Publish

Rewrite your informational survey in your best handwriting or on a computer. Look at Shi-Mei's information survey on page 9 for ideas. Add a photograph or drawing if you want. Present your informational survey to the class.

✓ **Editing Checklist**

me	my partner	
❑	❑	used articles, numbers, and adjectives correctly
❑	❑	used simple present tense with *be* and subject pronouns correctly
❑	❑	used correct spelling, punctuation, and capitalization

TECHNOLOGY

Searching with Keywords

Do a keyword search. Go to an Internet search engine. Type your complete school name. Click SEARCH . Do any other schools have the same name? Click on a hyperlink for a school. Write down the school address. Do this for three schools.

Unit 2

Describe Your Family and Home

UNIT OBJECTIVES

Writing
descriptive writing

Organization
spatial order

Writing Strategies
complete sentences

Vocabulary
home and family (singular/plural)
adjectives
action verbs

Grammar
simple present tense
have/has
prepositions
possessive form

Technology
citing Internet sources

My Family Album

Mark Hanson

My name is (1) Mark Hanson .
I'm fifteen years old.
I live in (2) .

This is my father.
He (3)
in a restaurant.
His name is Mike.
He (4)
in his free time.

My (7)
name is Alex.
He's a student.
(8) funny.
He (9)
in his free time.

My mother is very smart.
(5) is Janet.
She's a (6) .

Our house has (10) rooms.
It has a living room, a kitchen, a bathroom,
and two bedrooms.
My bedroom is (11) the
kitchen.
My bedroom is big, but it is not
(12) !

A Discuss. Complete the information. Compare answers with a partner.

1. I have [2] people in my family.

2. Their names are
[MAX CRUZ]
[NOEL PINTO]
[ ]

3. I live in ... (circle the word)
a house   (an apartment)

4. My home has... (write numbers)
[3] bedroom(s)   [1] living room(s)
[2] bathroom(s)   [1] kitchen
[1] other room(s)

5. My home is... (circle the words)
big   small   (comfortable)
(nice)   (clean)

B Read. Read the description.

Francisco's Family

Francisco has four people in his family. His parents' names are Berta and Miguel. Francisco does not have a brother. He has a sister. Her name is Maria. Francisco's father is very smart. He is a computer programmer. He works in a big office. Francisco's mother works in a bookstore. She is very kind. She reads books in her free time. Francisco and Maria do not work. They go to Oak Street School. They are good students. They study every day. After school, Francisco plays baseball. Maria listens to music.

Francisco and his family live at 145 Oak Street in Los Angeles, California. They do not live in a house. They have a nice apartment. Their apartment has three bedrooms, a living room, a kitchen, and a bathroom. Mr. and Mrs. Garcia's bedroom is next to the living room. Maria's bedroom is next to their room. Francisco's bedroom is across from Maria's bedroom. The bathroom is between Francisco's bedroom and Maria's bedroom. They aren't big bedrooms. They are small. They are clean and comfortable. The Garcia family is very happy in their home.

Learn new words. Write them in your personal dictionary.

C Write captions. Write a sentence for each picture on page 15. Use sentences from the reading.

1. Francisco has four people in his family.

2. _____

3. _____

4. _____

5. _____

6. _____

The Garcia Family
145 Oak Street
Los Angeles CA 90802

7. _____

Oak Street Apartments

8. _____

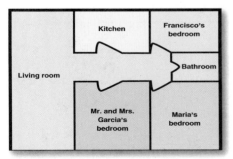

Kitchen | Francisco's bedroom
Living room | Bathroom
Mr. and Mrs. Garcia's bedroom | Maria's bedroom

9. _____

10. _____

Unit 2   Describe Your Family and Home   **15**

VOCABULARY

A Complete the sentences. Use the singular and plural nouns from the box.

bedrooms	mother	living room	kitchen	father	~~parents~~
bathroom	sister	house		brother	apartment

1. Berta and Miguel are Francisco's _____parents_____.

2. Maria is Francisco's _____.

3. Francisco is Maria's _____.

4. Francisco's _____ is a computer programmer.

5. His _____ works in a bookstore.

6. The Garcia family lives in an _____.

7. They do not live in a _____.

8. Their apartment has three _____.

9. It also has a living room, a _____, and a bathroom.

10. Francisco's parents' bedroom is next to the _____.

11. The _____ is between Francisco's room and Maria's room.

Remember!
Nouns can be singular (*one*) or plural (*more than one*). To make most nouns plural, add an *s* or *es* after the singular noun.

Singular	Plural
one bedroom	**two** bedrooms
one class	**three** classes

B These sentences are incorrect. Rewrite the sentences. Use the correct adjectives from page 14.

Remember!
Adjectives are sometimes after the verb *be*.
   Mr. Garcia **is smart**.

Adjectives are sometimes before a noun.
   They aren't **big bedrooms**.

1. Mr. Garcia is *silly*.   Mr. Garcia is smart. _____

2. Mr. Garcia works in a *small* office. _____

3. Mrs. Garcia is very *mean*. _____

4. Francisco and Maria are *bad* students. _____

5. The apartment has *big* bedrooms. _____

6. The apartment is *dirty*. _____

7. The Garcias are *sad*. _____

C Unscramble the verbs from the reading on page 14.

1. veli   _____live_____

2. kwro   _____

3. dare   _____

4. og   _____

5. yalp   _____

6. siltne   _____

7. sytdu   _____

GRAMMAR

➤ Learn more in the Grammar Reference, pages 131–141.

Sentences with the Simple Present Tense		
	Affirmative	**Negative**
most verbs	Francisco **lives** on Oak Street. Mr. and Mrs. Garcia **live** in an apartment.	He **does not live** on Elm Street. They **do not live** in a house.
have and **has**	Francisco **has** a small bedroom. Mr. and Mrs. Garcia **have** a clean bedroom.	He **does not have** a big bedroom. They **do not have** a dirty bedroom.

Contractions
doesn't = does not
don't = do not

A Write affirmative or negative statements. Use the correct form of the verb.

1. Francisco (has / have) four people in his family.

   Francisco has four people in his family.

2. Francisco (doesn't have / don't have) a brother.

   _____

3. Mrs. Garcia (reads / read) books in her free time.

   _____

4. Francisco and Maria (doesn't work / don't work).

   _____

5. They (goes / go) to school.

   _____

6. They (studies / study) every day.

   _____

7. Francisco (plays / play) baseball after school.

   _____

8. Maria (listens / listen) to music after school.

   _____

9. Francisco and Maria (doesn't live / don't live) at 115 Oak Street in Los Angeles, California.

   _____

10. They (has / have) six rooms in their apartment.

   _____

Prepositions

The bedroom is **next to** the kitchen.
The kitchen is **across from** their bedroom.
The bathroom is **between** his bedroom and her bedroom.

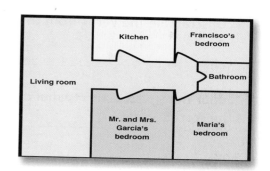

B Complete the sentences. You may use prepositions more than once.

1. Mr. and Mrs. Garcia's bedroom is _____ next to _____ the living room.
2. The kitchen is _ACROSS FROM_ their bedroom.
3. Maria's bedroom is _NEXT TO_ her parents' bedroom.
4. Francisco's bedroom is _NEXT TO_ Maria's bedroom.
5. The bathroom is _BETWEEN_ Francisco's bedroom and Maria's bedroom.

Possessive Form

Noun + 's	Possessive Adjectives
Francisco's bedroom is across from **Maria's** bedroom.	**His** bedroom is across from **her** bedroom.
Mr. and Mrs. Garcia's bedroom is next to the living room.	**Their** bedroom is next to the living room.

C Rewrite the sentences. Change the possessive form.

1. *Mr. Garcia's* office is very big.
   His office is very big.

2. *Mrs. Garcia's* job is in a bookstore.
   Her job is in a bookstore.

3. The school is close to *Francisco and Maria's* apartment.
   The school is close to their apartment.

4. *Their* bedroom is next to the living room.
   _____

5. *His* bedroom is next to the kitchen.
   Francisco's bedroom is next to the kitchen

6. *His* bedroom is across from *her* bedroom.
   _____

ORGANIZATION

Spatial Order

Number the sentences in spatial order. Then write the sentences in the correct order.

Remember!
You can use spatial order to describe a place. Spatial order gives information by location, or space. Look at page 14. The writer describes Mr. and Mrs. Garcia's room first. Then the writer describes the rooms near their room. This helps the reader to "see" the apartment.

Group 1

_____ Maria's bedroom is next to her parents' room.

__1__ The Garcia family's apartment has a large living room.

_____ Francisco's bedroom is across from Maria's bedroom.

__2__ Mr. and Mrs. Garcia's bedroom is next to the living room.

1. The Garcia family's apartment has a large living room.

Group 2

__3__ The kitchen is across from his parents' room.

_____ His parents' room is between Maria's bedroom and the living room.

__1__ Francisco's bedroom is small.

_____ His bedroom is next to the kitchen.

WRITING STRATEGIES

Complete Sentences

Remember!
A complete sentence has a subject and a verb. The subject tells who or what the sentence is about. The verb tells the action of the subject. See page 137 for more about sentences.

Francisco and his family live at 145 Oak Street.

       SUBJECT   VERB

Rewrite the sentences. Circle the subject and underline the verb in each sentence.

1. (Mr. Garcia) works in a big office.

2. (Francisco's) mother works in a bookstore.

3. (She) reads books in her free time.

4. (Francisco and Maria) go to Oak Street School.

5. (They) study every day.

6. (Francisco) plays baseball.

7. (Maria) listens to music.

(Mr. Garcia) works in a big office.

Descriptive Writing

Descriptive writing gives details and information about a topic. A narrative description describes a part of your life, like your home or family. Stories often use descriptive writing.

 A **Read.** Read Mark's description of his family.

Learn new words. Write them in your personal dictionary.

My Home and Family

Mark Hanson

My name is Mark Hanson. I'm fifteen years old. I live in Houston, Texas. My father works in a restaurant. His name is Mike. He listens to music in his free time. My mother is very smart. Her name is Janet. She's a teacher. My brother's name is Alex. He's a student. He's funny. He plays soccer in his free time.

Our family lives in a nice house. Our house has five rooms. It has a living room, a kitchen, a bathroom, and two bedrooms. The living room is very big. The kitchen is next to the living room. My bedroom is across from the kitchen. My brother and I share a bedroom. Our bedroom is big, but it is not clean! Our house is very comfortable. My family is very happy here.

  B **Write words and phrases.** Complete the information for Mark's family album on page 21. Use words and phrases from his description.

My Family Album

Mark Hanson

My name is (1) Mark Hanson .

I'm fifteen years old.

I live in (2) HOUSTON .

This is my father.

He (3) WORKS

in a restaurant.

His name is Mike.

He (4) LISTENS TO MUSIC

in his free time.

My (7) BROTHER

name is Alex.

He's a student.

(8) HE'S funny.

He (9) PLAYS SOCCER

in his free time.

My mother is very smart.

(5) ~~She~~ Her NAME is Janet.

She's a (6) TEACHER .

Our house has (10) FIVE rooms.

It has a living room, a kitchen, a bathroom,
and two bedrooms.

My bedroom is (11) ACROSS FROM the
kitchen.

My bedroom is big, but it is not

(12) CLEAN !

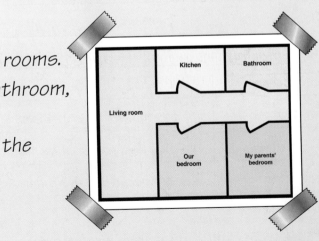

Kitchen | Bathroom
Living room
Our bedroom | My parents' bedroom

STEP-BY-STEP WRITING

Purpose: Describe Your Family and Home

WRITING PROMPT

Make a family album. Describe yourself, your family, and your home. Write two or more sentences about each. Include photos or drawings.

STEP 1 Pre-write

Look at Mark's web organizers. Think about the information you need for your family album. Make web organizers about your home and family:

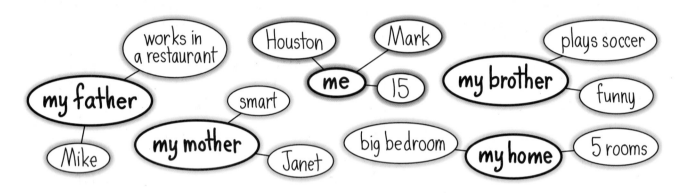

Mark's Web Organizers

STEP 2 Organize

Look at Mark's sentence organizer. Organize your notes into sentences. Write sentences about you, your family, and your home.

Mark's Sentence Organizer	
Topic	Sentences
me	My name is Mark Hanson. I am ….
my father	He works in a restaurant. His name is …
my mother	My mother is very smart. My mother's name is …
my brother	He plays soccer in his free time. He is a …
my home	Our house has five rooms. My bedroom is …

STEP 3 Draft and Revise

A | **Practice.** Look at Mark's first draft. How can he improve it? Answer the questions.

Mark's First Draft	
me:	(1) My name is Mark Hanson. (2) I'm fifteen years old. (3) I live in Houston, Texas.
my father:	(4) He works in a restaurant. (5) His name is Mike.
	(6) He listens to music in his free time.
my mother:	(7) My mother is very smart. (8) My mother's name is Janet.
	(9) My mother is a teacher.
my brother:	(10) I have a brother. (11) His name is Alex. (12) He's a student. (13) He's funny.
	(14) He plays soccer in his free time.
my home:	(15) Our house has five rooms. (16) My bedroom is across from the kitchen.
	(17) My bedroom is big. (18) It is not clean!

1. What sentence should Mark add before sentence 4?
   Ⓐ This is my father.
   B This is Mark.
   C He lives in Houston, Texas.
   D My father's name is Mike.

2. What is another way to write sentence 8?
   A Her mother's name is Janet.
   B Janet is her mother's name.
   C My name is Janet.
   D Her name is Janet.

3. What is the best way to combine sentences 10 and 11?
   A My brother has a name.
   B My name is Alex.
   C My brother's name is Alex.
   D This is Alex.

4. Where can Mark add this sentence?
It has a living room, a kitchen, a bathroom, and two bedrooms.
   A after Sentence 14
   B after Sentence 15
   C after Sentence 16
   D It doesn't fit.

B | **Draft.** Write a first draft for your family album. Use your notes from Steps 1 and 2.

C | **Revise.** Read your first draft. How can you improve it? Look at the revision checklist. Revise your writing.

☑ **Revision Checklist**

❑ I described myself, my family, and my home.

❑ I wrote two or more sentences about myself.

❑ I wrote two or more sentences about each person in my family.

❑ I wrote two or more sentences about my home.

STEP 4 Edit

A | **Practice.** Look at the sentences. Choose the best substitute for the underlined words. If the sentence is correct, choose "Make no change."

1. Mary's sister is really <u>mean</u>. I like her a lot!
   A uncomfortable
   B sad
   Ⓒ nice
   D Make no change.

2. The bedroom is <u>across from</u> the kitchen.
   A across to
   B between
   C next from
   D Make no change.

3. Paul and John <u>goes</u> to Central High School.
   A go
   B does go
   C doesn't go
   D Make no change.

4. <u>Maria's bedroom is next to Mark's bedroom.</u>
   A Their bedroom is next to his bedroom.
   B His bedroom is next to their bedroom.
   C Her bedroom is next to his bedroom.
   D Make no change.

5. <u>My father in a music store.</u>
   A My works in a music store.
   B My father next to a music store.
   C My father works in a music store.
   D Make no change.

B | **Edit.** Reread your draft from Step 3. Look at the editing checklist. Edit your writing.

 C | **Peer Edit.** Exchange drafts with a partner. Tell your partner what you like about the draft. Look at the editing checklist. Tell your partner how to improve the draft.

STEP 5 Publish

Make your family album. Write it in your notebook or on a computer. Look at Mark's album on page 21 for ideas. Remember to include a title and your photos or drawings. Present your family album to the class.

✔️ Editing Checklist

me	my partner	
❏	❏	used family words and adjectives correctly
❏	❏	used correct verb tenses, prepositions, and possessive forms
❏	❏	used complete sentences
❏	❏	used correct spelling, punctuation, and capitalization

TECHNOLOGY

Citing Internet Sources

Cite Internet **sources.**
Include the following:

WEB PAGE TITLE   WEB SITE NAME   PUBLICATION DATE

"Baby names." Social Security Administration. 29 May 2006.
<http://www.ssa.gov/OACT/babynames/>. (17 April 2007).

URL   ACCESS DATE

 Go to an Internet search engine. Type "Heinle's Newbury House Dictionary." Click `SEARCH`. Click on the hyperlink for "Heinle's Newbury House Dictionary of American English." Look up the word *family*. Write the definitions in your personal dictionary. Cite the Internet source.

GROUP WRITING

Work together to write sentences about Melinda or Greg.

1. Choose Melinda or Greg.
2. Read the person's information.
3. Tell your teacher about the person.
4. Your teacher writes sentences.
5. Revise and edit the sentences with the class.
6. Copy the sentences.

Informational Survey

First Name: Melinda
Last Name: Peterson
Nickname: Mel
Age: 14
City/State: Miami, Florida
English Teacher: Mrs. Lee
Teacher Description: Nice and friendly
School Name: South High School
School Address: 1624 8th Avenue Northeast, Miami Florida
School Description: Big and colorful

My name is Greg Mandel.
I am fifteen years old.
I live at 16 West 7th Steet
in Chicago, Illinois. I am
a student. In my free time,
I play soccer.

My father's name is William.
He is a teacher. He plays golf in his free time.
My mom is really funny. Her name is Karen.
She works in an office.

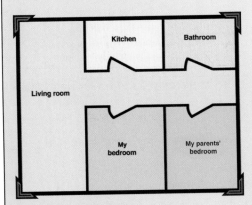

Kitchen   Bathroom

Living room

My bedroom   My parents' bedroom

Our house has a living room, a kitchen,
a bathroom, and two bedrooms.
My bedroom is next to my parents' room
The bathroom is across from my room.
My bedroom is very cool. It is very colorful.
I like my home a lot.

TIMED WRITING

Choose one writing task. Complete the task in 45 minutes.

WRITING PROMPT 1

What are you like? Write about yourself, your school, and your family. Write three or more sentences about each topic.

WRITING PROMPT 2

A "dream home" is the perfect home for you. Draw a picture of your dream home. Give an address. Describe your dream home. Label the rooms. Tell where the rooms are located.

> **Test Tip**
> **Don't rush!** Always read the writing prompt carefully.
>
> <u>Underline</u> or (circle) important words. This helps you understand the prompt better.

SELF-CHECK

Think about your writing skills. Check (✔) the answers that are true.

1. I understand....
   - ❑ classroom words.
   - ❑ home, and family words.

2. I can correctly use...
   - ❑ articles.
   - ❑ singular and plural nouns.
   - ❑ adjectives.
   - ❑ action verbs.

3. I can correctly use...
   - ❑ the simple present tense.
   - ❑ subject pronouns.
   - ❑ prepositions.
   - ❑ the possessive form.

4. I remember to capitalize...
   - ❑ the first word in a sentence.
   - ❑ the names of people and places.
   - ❑ languages.
   - ❑ important words in titles.

5. I can...
   - ❑ write complete sentences.
   - ❑ find the subject and verb in a sentence.

6. I can organize my writing by...
   - ❑ topic.
   - ❑ location or space.

7. I can write to...
   - ❑ inform a reader.
   - ❑ describe.

Unit 3

Explain How to Do Something

UNIT OBJECTIVES

Writing
technical writing

Organization
sequential order with
  sequence words

Writing Conventions
end punctuation

Vocabulary
foods
action verbs

Grammar
imperative statements
count and noncount nouns

Technology
narrowing a keyword search

AL'S SUPERMARKET
SALE SATURDAY!

How to Make Chicken Sal
Lisha Martin

First, buy some cooked (1) _chicken_ ,
some mayonnaise, some (2) _____ ,
one tomato, one (3) _____ , and
some (4) _____ and pepper.

(5) _____
Ask an adult to help.

(6) _____

(7) _____

(8) _____
Put the tomato and
onion in the bowl.

(9) _____

(10) _____
Finally, put the
lettuce on a plate.

A **Discuss.** Answer the questions. Compare answers with a partner.

> **1.** What fruit do you like? Check (✔) the items or add your own.
>
> ☐ apples ☐ bananas ☐ oranges other: _____
>
> **2.** What vegetables do you like? Check (✔) the items or add your own.
>
> ☐ tomatoes ☐ lettuce ☐ onions other: _____
>
> **3.** Do you eat...?
>
> ☐ meat ☐ chicken ☐ fish other: _____
>
> **4.** Do you have a supermarket near your home?
>
> ☐ yes ☐ no

 B **Read.** Read the passage about the Garcia family.

Learn new words. Write them in your personal dictionary.

Grocery Shopping

The Garcia family goes grocery shopping every Saturday. They go to Al's Supermarket. It is near their apartment. It is very convenient. Francisco and Maria often go grocery shopping with their parents. First, the family walks into the supermarket. Then, Francisco gets a shopping cart. Next, Mrs. Garcia reads the shopping list. She tells Maria, "Buy two tomatoes." She tells Mr. Garcia, "Get six onions. Don't forget the bread." After that, Mr. Garcia and Maria get the groceries. The shopping list is very long! The Garcia family needs a lot of things. They buy vegetables, fruit, meat, eggs, and cheese. They don't buy junk food. The Garcia family likes healthy food. Mrs. Garcia is a great cook. Next, Mrs. Garcia pays for the groceries and the Garcia family goes home. Then, Maria and Francisco carry the groceries into the apartment. There are many bags. Mr. and Mrs. Garcia put away the groceries. Finally, the Garcia family relaxes and eats lunch!

 C **Write captions.** Write a sentence for each picture on page 29. Use sentences from the reading.

1. The Garcia family goes grocery shopping every Saturday.

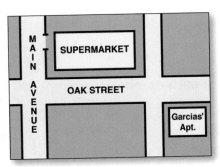

2. _____

3. _____

4. _____

5. _____

6. _____

7. _____

8. _____

9. _____

10. _____

11. _____

12. _____

VOCABULARY

A Write the correct food next to each number.

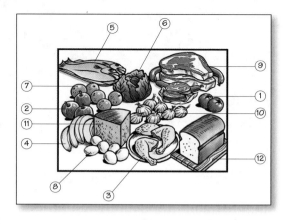

oranges	lettuce	meat	chicken
onions	bananas	eggs	bread
~~tomatoes~~	apples	fish	cheese

1. ___tomatoes___   5. _____   9. _____

2. _____   6. _____   10. _____

3. _____   7. _____   11. _____

4. _____   8. _____   12. _____

B Complete the sentences with action verbs from the box. Use the correct form of the simple present tense.

like	buy	pay	~~go~~	get	relax
walk	tell	carry	put	eat	

1. The Garcia family ___goes___ grocery shopping every Saturday.

2. First, the family _____ into the supermarket.

3. Francisco _____ a shopping cart.

4. Mrs. Garcia _____ Maria, "Buy two tomatoes."

5. They _____ vegetables, fruit, and cheese.

6. The Garcia family _____ healthy food.

7. Mrs. Garcia _____ for the groceries.

8. Maria and Francisco _____ the groceries into the apartment.

9. Mr. and Mrs. Garcia _____ away the groceries.

10. Finally, the Garcia family _____.

11. Then they _____ lunch.

GRAMMAR

▶ Learn more in the Grammar Reference, pages 131–141.

Imperative Sentences		
Simple Present	**Imperative (Affirmative)**	**Imperative (Negative)**
You get six onions. **You go** to the supermarket.	**Get** six onions. **Go** to the supermarket.	**Don't get** six onions. **Don't go** to the supermarket.

A Write the words in the correct order to make imperative sentences.

1. to / the / go / supermarket _Go to the supermarket._

2. a / cart / shopping / get _____

3. and / buy / eggs / fruit _____

4. home / go _____

5. the / groceries / carry _____

6. groceries / the / away / put _____

B Change the sentences in Exercise A to the negative imperative form.

1. _Don't go to the supermarket._ _____

2. _____

3. _____

4. _____

5. _____

6. _____

Count and Noncount Nouns		
Count Nouns **Singular**	**Plural**	**Noncount** Nouns **No Specific Amount**
a banana **an** orange **the** egg	**three** bananas **five** oranges **the** eggs	**some** bread **some** meat **some** lettuce
Count nouns are singular or plural.		Noncount nouns don't have plural forms.

C Write the foods from Vocabulary Exercise A on page 30 in the correct column.

Count	Noncount
_____ tomatoes _____	_____
_____	_____
_____	_____
_____	_____
_____	_____

D Write a sentence for each food. Use the imperative form of *buy*. Remember to use an article, a number, or *some*.

1. Buy two tomatoes. _____

2. _____

3. _____

4. _____

5. _____

6. _____

7. _____

8. _____

9. _____

10. _____

11. _____

12. _____

ORGANIZATION

Sequential Order with Sequence Words

Number the sentences in sequential order. Then, write the sentences in the correct order.

Group 1

_____ Next, Mrs. Garcia reads the shopping list.

__1__ First, the Garcias go to the supermarket.

_____ After that, Maria and Mr. Garcia go get the groceries.

_____ Then, Francisco gets a shopping cart.

First, the Garcias go to the supermarket.

Group 2

_____ Finally, the family relaxes and has lunch.

_____ Next, Mr. and Mrs. Garcia put away the groceries in the kitchen.

_____ Mrs. Garcia pays for the groceries and the Garcia family goes home.

_____ Then, Maria and Francisco carry the groceries into the apartment.

WRITING CONVENTIONS

End Punctuation

Write the sentences. Add the correct end punctuation mark.

1. (statement) The Garcia family goes grocery shopping every Saturday
2. (question) Do they go to Al's Supermarket
3. (question) Is it near their apartment
4. (strong statement) The shopping list is very long
5. (statement) Mrs. Garcia is a great cook
6. (strong statement) Finally, the family relaxes and eats lunch

1. *The Garcia family goes grocery shopping every Saturday.*

2.

Technical Writing

Technical writing often gives instructions. It sometimes explains how to do a procedure. Recipes and directions are examples of technical writing.

 A **Read.** Read Lisha's recipe for making chicken salad.

Lisha's Chicken Salad

  Learn new words. Write them in your personal dictionary.

Ingredients:

cooked chicken   1 tomato   mayonnaise
1 onion   lettuce   salt and pepper

Directions:

First, buy the ingredients. Ask an adult to help. Next, cut the chicken into small pieces. Put the chicken in a bowl. Then, add the mayonnaise. After that, cut the tomato and the onion into small pieces. Put the tomato and onion in the bowl. Next, add some salt and pepper. Finally, put the lettuce on a plate. Put the chicken salad on the lettuce. Then eat and enjoy!

 B **Write words and sentences.** Complete the information for Lisha's recipe poster on page 35. Use words and sentences from Lisha's recipe.

A Recipe Poster

How to Make Chicken Salad

Lisha Martin

First, buy some cooked (1) _chicken_ , some mayonnaise, some (2) _____, one tomato, one (3) _____, and some (4) _____ and pepper.

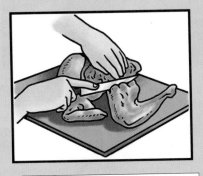

(5) _____

(6) _____

(7) _____

Ask an adult to help.

(8) _____

Put the tomato and onion in the bowl.

(9) _____

Finally, put the lettuce on a plate.

(10) _____

STEP-BY-STEP WRITING

Purpose: Explain How to Do Something

WRITING PROMPT

Make a recipe poster. List your ingredients. Divide your recipe into steps. Give instructions for each step. Use sequence words. Include pictures of your instructions.

STEP 1 Pre-write

Look at Lisha's notes. Think about the information you need for your recipe poster. Write notes.

Lisha's Notes

Topic	Details
recipe name	Chicken Salad
ingredients	cooked chicken, mayonnaise, ...
instructions	buy ingredients, cut chicken, add mayo...

STEP 2 Organize

Look at Lisha's organizer. Categorize your notes into steps. Copy the chart or make one on a computer. Add steps if you need to. Complete the organizer with instructions for your recipe.

Lisha's Organizer

Step 1
Buy the ingredients.

Step 2
Cut the chicken into...

Step 3
Add the...

Step 4

Step 5

Step 6

STEP 3 Draft and Revise

A **Practice.** Look at Lisha's first draft. How can she improve it? Answer the questions.

Lisha's First Draft	
Step 1:	First, buy the ingredients.
Step 2:	Next, cut the chicken into small pieces.
Step 3:	Add the mayonnaise.
Step 4:	After that, cut the tomato and the onion into small pieces. Put the tomato and onion in the bowl.
Step 5:	Next, put some salt and pepper.
Step 6:	Finally, put the lettuce on a plate. Put the chicken salad on the lettuce.

1. What is the best way to add details to Step 1?
   A First, buy some ingredients.
   B First, buy an ingredient.
   C First, buy some chicken, some mayonnaise, some lettuce, some tomato, some onion, and some salt and pepper.
   D First, buy some chicken, some mayonnaise, some lettuce, one tomato, one onion, and some salt and pepper.

2. Where can Lisha add this instruction?
   Put the chicken in a bowl.
   A after Step 1
   B after Step 2
   C after Step 3
   D It doesn't fit.

3. What sequence word can Lisha add to Step 3?
   A First,
   B Then,
   C Finally,
   D After,

4. What is the best way to improve Step 5?
   A Change *put* to *cut.*
   B Change *put* to *buy.*
   C Change *put* to *add.*
   D Change *put* to *eat.*

B **Draft.** Write a first draft for your recipe poster. Use your notes from Steps 1 and 2.

C **Revise.** Read your first draft. How can you improve it? Look at the revision checklist. Revise your writing.

Revision Checklist
- ❏ I listed my ingredients.
- ❏ I divided my recipe into steps.
- ❏ I gave clear instructions for each step.
- ❏ I used sequence words correctly.

STEP 4 Edit

A **Practice.** Look at the sentences. Choose the best word or phrase to complete each sentence.

1. Buy six _____.
   A some tomato
   B tomatos
   C some tomatoes
   (D) tomatoes

2. Cut an apple. Put _____ apple in a bowl.
   A an
   B the
   C a
   D some

3. Don't _____ lettuce. We have a lot.
   A carry
   B add
   C cut
   D buy

4. Does Marta go shopping on _____.
   A Saturdays.
   B Saturdays!
   C Saturdays?
   D Saturdays,

5. Get _____ bread at the store.
   A many
   B six
   C some
   D a

B **Edit.** Reread your draft from Step 3. Look at the editing checklist. Edit your writing.

C **Peer Edit.** Exchange drafts with a partner. Tell your partner what you like about the draft. Look at the editing checklist. Tell your partner how to improve the draft.

✔ Editing Checklist

me	my partner	
❑	❑	used imperatives correctly
❑	❑	used count and noncount nouns correctly
❑	❑	used correct spelling, punctuation, and capitalization

STEP 5 Publish

Make your recipe poster. Write in your best handwriting or design it on a computer. Look at Lisha's poster on page 35 for ideas. Remember to include a title, your name, and pictures of your instructions. Present your poster to the class.

TECHNOLOGY

Narrowing a Keyword Search

Hits are the **Web sites** you find in a search. Do a **keyword search** for *chicken salad*. How many hits did you get? Write down the number of hits. Do a **keyword search** for *"chicken salad."* Use **quotation marks** (" "). Look at the difference between the numbers. Quotation marks find an exact phrase.

 Do a **keyword search** for *"recipe ingredients"* and a favorite food. Click on a hyperlink to find a recipe. Write down the ingredients. Cite the Internet source.

Unit 4

Write about a Holiday or Celebration

UNIT OBJECTIVES

Writing
expository writing

Organization
order of importance

Writing Strategies
sentence combining with
    signal and connecting words

Vocabulary
celebration words
months and ordinal numbers
countries and nationalities

Grammar
wh- questions and answers
prepositional phrases
adverbs of frequency

Technology
expanding a keyword search

DECEMBER 3
Francisco's birthday!

★ MY FAVORITE H...
Irene Leska

JULY
Sun	Mon	Tue	Wed	Thur	Fri	Sat
	1	2	3	4	5	6
7	8	9	10	11	12	13
14	15	16	17	18	19	20
21	22	23	24	25	26	27
28	29	30	31			

1. American Independence Day celebrates the freedom of the United States from England.

2.

3.

4.

5.

6.

A Discuss. Ask and answer the questions with a partner. Share your partner's answers with the class.

1. What's your favorite holiday or celebration? ❏ my birthday ❏ New Year's Eve
   ❏ Thanksgiving ❏ other: _____

2. When is the celebration? _____

3. Where do you celebrate? ❏ at home ❏ at a restaurant ❏ at a parade
   ❏ other: _____

4. How do you celebrate? ❏ I sing. ❏ I dance. ❏ I eat special foods.
   ❏ I wear special clothes. ❏ other: _____

5. Who celebrates with you? ❏ family ❏ friends ❏ other: _____

6. Why do you like this holiday or celebration? _____

Learn new words. Write them in your personal dictionary.

B Read. Read the passage about favorite celebrations.

Let's Celebrate!

Today is Francisco's favorite celebration. It's December 3. It's Francisco's birthday. He is 16 years old today. Francisco's family never forgets his birthday. They always have a birthday party at their apartment. Francisco's friends and family usually come to the party. They play games and eat birthday cake. Francisco usually gets a lot of nice presents, too. He likes his birthday because it's fun.

Maria's favorite holiday is New Year's Eve. New Year's Eve is on December 31. It is the last night before the new year. Maria usually celebrates New Year's Eve at home. Maria's family often celebrates New Year's Eve with her. On New Year's Eve, Maria yells "Happy New Year!" at midnight. Maria thinks New Year's Eve is exciting.

Mr. and Mrs. Garcia like *Cinco de Mayo*. Mr. Garcia is Mexican. He's from Puebla, Mexico. *Cinco de Mayo* is a traditional holiday in Puebla, but it's very popular in the U.S. as well. *Cinco de Mayo* is on May 5. The Garcia family often goes to the *Cinco de Mayo* parade in Los Angeles. At the parade, people usually sing or dance. People sometimes wear special green, red, and white clothes, too. Mr. and Mrs. Garcia like *Cinco de Mayo* because it's enjoyable.

C Write captions. Write a sentence for each picture on page 41.
Use sentences from the reading.

1. It's December 3. _____

2. _____

3. _____

4. _____

5. _____

6. _____

7. _____

8. _____

9. _____

10. _____

VOCABULARY

A Complete the sentences with words from the box.
Use each word only once.

popular	~~birthday~~	party	celebrates	dance
presents	special	traditional	holiday	parade

1. Francisco's _____birthday_____ is December 3.

2. Francisco's family always has a _____ for his birthday.

3. Francisco usually gets a lot of nice _____ for his birthday.

4. Maria's favorite _____ is New Year's Eve.

5. Maria _____ New Year's Eve at home.

6. *Cinco de Mayo* is a _____ celebration in Puebla, Mexico.

7. It is very _____ in the U.S., too. People really like it.

8. The Garcia family often goes to the *Cinco de Mayo* _____ in Los Angeles.

9. At the parade, people usually sing or _____.

10. People sometimes wear _____ red,
    green, and white clothes.

B Write the months in order.

November	April	~~January~~	June	March	February
May	July	December	August	September	October

1. _____January_____   7. _____

2. _____   8. _____

3. _____   9. _____

4. _____   10. _____

5. _____   11. _____

6. _____   12. _____

C Complete the chart with the correct country
or nationality.

Country	Nationality / Adjective Form
Mexico	Mexican
	American
the United Kingdom (U.K.)	British
Haiti	
	Cuban
	Chinese
Vietnam	
	Indian
Korea	
	Brazilian

GRAMMAR

➤ Learn more in the Grammar Reference,
pages 131–141.

Wh- Questions

Wh- Questions	Complete Answers
Who celebrates Francisco's birthday with him?	Francisco's family celebrates his birthday with him.
What is Mr. Garcia's favorite holiday?	Mr. Garcia's favorite holiday is *Cinco de Mayo*.
When is Francisco's birthday?	Francisco's birthday is on December 3.
Where is Mr. Garcia from?	Mr. Garcia is from Puebla, Mexico.
Why does Maria like New Year's Eve?	Maria thinks New Year's Eve is exciting.
How does the Garcia family celebrate Francisco's birthday?	The Garcia family has a birthday party to celebrate Francisco's birthday.

A Complete the *wh-* questions. Then write complete answers. Use the information
in parentheses.

1. Q: _____Where_____ is Francisco's birthday party?

   A: (at his apartment) Francisco's birthday party is at his apartment. _____

2. Q: _____ is *Cinco de Mayo*?

   A: (May 5) _____

3. Q: _____ celebrates New Year's Eve with Maria?

   A: (Maria's family) _____

4. Q: _____ is Mr. Garcia's favorite holiday?

   A: (*Cinco de Mayo*) _____

5. Q: _____ does the Garcia family celebrate *Cinco de Mayo*?

   A: (go to the parade) _____

6. Q: _____ does Francisco like his birthday?

   A: (it's fun) _____

Prepositional Phrases

Prepositional Phrase	Example
Time **on** [a day OR date] **in** [a month]	Maria stays up late **on New Year's Eve.** New Year's Eve is **on December 31.** Francisco's birthday is **in December.**
Location **in** [a place OR country] **at** [a place OR event]	*Cinco de Mayo* is very popular **in the U.S.** Francisco celebrates his birthday **at home.**
Direction **to** [a place]	The Garcia family goes **to the Cinco de Mayo parade.**

B   Complete the sentences with *in, on, at,* or *to.*

1. Francisco's birthday is _____on_____ December 3.

2. Francisco's friends usually come _____ his apartment.

3. Francisco always has fun _____ his birthday.

4. Maria yells "Happy New Year!" _____ New Year's Eve.

5. New Year's Eve is _____ December.

6. *Cinco de Mayo* is a traditional holiday _____ Puebla, Mexico.

7. People sing or dance _____ the parade.

Adverbs of Frequency

always	usually	often	sometimes	never

100% ◄————————————————————————► 0%
of the time   of the time

C   Complete the sentences. Use the correct adverbs from the reading on page 40.

1. Francisco's family _____never_____ forgets his birthday.

2. They _____ have a birthday party at their apartment.

3. Francisco's friends _____ come to the party.

4. Maria _____ celebrates New Year's Eve at home.

5. Maria _____ celebrates New Year's Eve with her family.

6. The Garcia family _____ goes to the *Cinco de Mayo* parade.

7. The people _____ wear special green, red, and white clothes.

Order of Importance

Remember!
Use questions to research a topic. Use complete answers to start writing. Organize the information in order of importance. Think about the topic and audience. Ask yourself "What is important for the audience to know first about the topic?"

A Write complete answers for the *wh-* questions. Use sentences from the reading on page 40.

Wh- Question	Complete Answer
What is Maria's favorite holiday?	1. Maria's favorite holiday is New Year's Eve.
Who celebrates with her?	2. _____
Where does she celebrate?	3. _____
When is the holiday?	4. _____
Why does she like it?	5. _____
How does she celebrate?	6. _____

B Write answers for the *wh-* questions. Use the complete answers from Exercise A. Then write the best title for the group of sentences.

(Title) _____

1. (What?) Maria's favorite holiday is New Year's Eve. _____

2. (When?) _____

3. (How?) _____

4. (Why?) _____

C Write the best title for the group of sentences in Exercise B.

Title 1: Maria's Favorite Holiday   **Title 2: How Maria Celebrates New Year's Eve**

WRITING STRATEGIES

Remember!
Use signal words like *too* and *as well* to add information.
Use connecting words like *or, but, and,* or *because* to connect ideas or sentences.

Sentence Combining

Change each sentence. Use the signal or connecting word in parentheses.

1. (and) Francisco's friends come to his party. Francisco's family comes to his party.
2. (and) They play games. They eat birthday cake.
3. (because) He likes his birthday. It's fun.
4. (as well) *Cinco de Mayo* is a holiday in Puebla, Mexico and it's popular in the U.S.
5. (or) At the parade, people usually sing. At the parade, people usually dance.

  1. Francisco's friends and family come to his party. _____

  2. _____

Expository Writing

Expository writing explains, describes, or gives information to an audience. Writers often research a topic to find information. Magazine articles and informational reports are examples of expository writing.

 A **Read.** Read Irene's magazine article about American Independence Day.

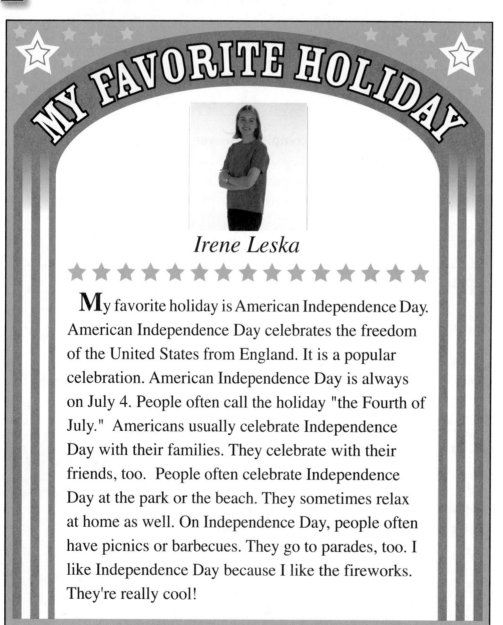

Learn new words. Write them in your personal dictionary.

MY FAVORITE HOLIDAY

Irene Leska

My favorite holiday is American Independence Day. American Independence Day celebrates the freedom of the United States from England. It is a popular celebration. American Independence Day is always on July 4. People often call the holiday "the Fourth of July." Americans usually celebrate Independence Day with their families. They celebrate with their friends, too. People often celebrate Independence Day at the park or the beach. They sometimes relax at home as well. On Independence Day, people often have picnics or barbecues. They go to parades, too. I like Independence Day because I like the fireworks. They're really cool!

 B **Write sentences.** Complete the information for Irene's celebration poster on page 47. Use words and sentences from her magazine article.

A Celebration Poster

⭐ MY FAVORITE HOLIDAY ⭐
Irene Leska

JULY						
Sun	Mon	Tue	Wed	Thur	Fri	Sat
	1	2	3	4	5	6
7	8	9	10	11	12	13
14	15	16	17	18	19	20
21	22	23	24	25	26	27
28	29	30	31			

1. *American Independence Day celebrates the freedom of the United States from England.*

2. _____

3. _____

4. _____

5. _____

6. _____

STEP-BY-STEP WRITING

Purpose: Write about a Holiday or Celebration

WRITING PROMPT

Make a celebration poster. Use *wh-* questions to research a favorite celebration. Write the complete answers to make your poster. Include a photograph or drawing for each answer.

☑ **Prompt Checklist**

- ☐ I read the prompt carefully.
- ☐ I understood what the prompt asks me to do.

STEP 1 Pre-write

Look at Irene's idea cluster. Copy the idea cluster or make one on a computer. Write the name of your celebration in the center. Complete the cluster with information about your celebration. Research any information you don't know.

Irene's Idea Cluster

STEP 2 Organize

Look at Irene's organizer. Organize your ideas. Copy the T-chart or make one on a computer. Complete a T-chart with sentences about your celebration.

Irene's T-chart	
Wh- Questions	**Complete Answers**
How do people celebrate?	People have barbecues or picnics on . . .
What is the celebration?	Our Independence Day is the celebration of . . .
When is the celebration?	Independence Day is on . . .
Who do people celebrate with?	Americans celebrate with . . .
Where do they celebrate?	People celebrate at the . . .
Why do I like the celebration?	I like fireworks . . .

STEP 3 Draft and Revise

A Practice. **Look at Irene's first draft. How can she improve it? Answer the questions.**

IRENE'S FIRST DRAFT

My Favorite Holiday

[first Picture]	1) People have barbecues or picnics on Independence Day.
[second Picture]	2) <u>Our Independence Day</u> celebrates the freedom of the United States from England.
[third Picture]	3) Independence Day is on July 4.
[fourth Picture]	4) Americans celebrate Independence Day with their families.
[fifth Picture]	5) People often celebrate Independence Day at the park or the beach.
[sixth Picture]	6) I like the fireworks because I like Independence Day.

1. What is important for the audience to know first about the topic?
   - Ⓐ Sentence 2
   - **B** Sentence 4
   - **C** Sentence 5
   - **D** Sentence 6

2. What is the best way to make the underlined part of sentence 2 more specific?
   - **A** Irene's Independence Day
   - **B** Their Independence Day
   - **C** American Independence Day
   - **D** United Independence Day

3. Where is the best place to add the adverb *usually* to sentence 4?
   - **A** before *celebrate*
   - **B** before *Independence*
   - **C** before *Day*
   - **D** before *with*

4. What's a better way to rewrite sentence 6?
   - **A** I like Independence Day but I like the fireworks.
   - **B** I like Independence Day because I like the fireworks.
   - **B** I like the fireworks because Independence Day.
   - **D** I like the fireworks or I like Independence Day.

B Draft. **Write a first draft for your celebration poster. Use your notes from Steps 1 and 2.**

C Revise. **Read your first draft. How can you improve it? Look at the revision checklist. Revise your writing.**

✓ Revision Checklist

- ❑ I explained what the celebration is.
- ❑ I wrote the date of the celebration.
- ❑ I wrote about who celebrates, where they celebrate, and how they celebrate.
- ❑ I explained why I like the celebration.

STEP 4 Edit

A **Practice. Look at the sentences. Choose the best word or phrase to complete each sentence.**

1. My mother's birthday is the _____ of May.
   A three
   B thirty
   Ⓒ third
   D thirteen

2. The _____ New Year celebration is very popular in San Francisco.
   A China
   B china
   C chinese
   D Chinese

3. I _____ watch the fireworks on the Fourth of July. I go every year.
   A always
   B don't

C never
D sometimes

4. My best friend's birthday is _____ April 16.
   A in
   B at
   C on
   D to

5. Mr. Simm's favorite holiday is _____.
   A Independence day
   B independence day
   C Independence Day
   D Independence Date

B **Edit. Reread your draft from Step 3. Look at the editing checklist. Edit your writing.**

C **Peer Edit. Exchange drafts with a partner. Tell your partner what you like about the draft. Look at the editing checklist. Tell your partner how to improve the draft.**

☑ Editing Checklist

me	my partner	
❑	❑	used dates, countries, and nationalities correctly
❑	❑	used adverbs of frequency and prepositions correctly
❑	❑	used correct spelling, punctuation, and capitalization

STEP 5 Publish

Make your celebration poster. Write it in your best handwriting or design it on a computer. Look at Irene's poster on page 47 for ideas. Remember to include a title, your name, and pictures of the celebration. Present your poster to the class.

TECHNOLOGY

Expanding a Keyword Search

Many countries have an Independence Day. Do a keyword search for the exact phrase "Independence Day celebration Vietnam" using quotation marks. What happens? You don't get many hits because your search is very narrow. Now search for the exact phrase "Independence Day celebration." Type the word *Vietnam* outside of the quotation marks. You get more hits because this expands the search.

Find five countries that celebrate an Independence Day. Make a list. Include the date of the celebration for each country. Cite your Internet sources.

GROUP WRITING

Work together to complete the information for one of the posters.

1. Look at the poster.
2. Discuss the pictures.
3. Tell your teacher about each picture.

4. Your teacher writes captions.
6. Copy the captions.

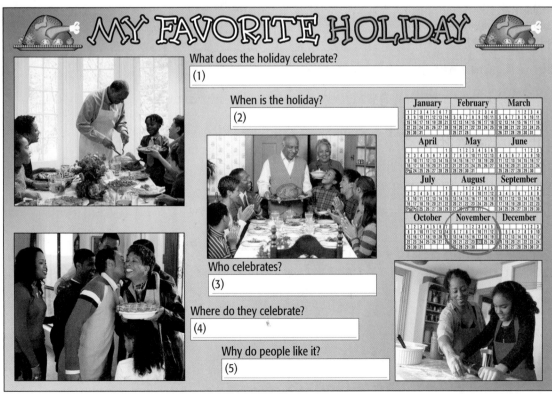

TIMED WRITING

Choose one writing prompt. Complete the writing task in 45 minutes.

WRITING PROMPT 1

Think about something you can do or make. Make a poster. Give instructions for each step. Use sequence words. Include pictures of your instructions.

WRITING PROMPT 2

Think about a popular free-time activity. Make a poster. Use *wh-* questions to guide your research and organization. Include pictures of the topic. Write complete sentences under the pictures to make your poster.

💡 Test Tip

Watch the time!
Total time: 45 minutes
Steps 1 & 2: pre-write, organize
 • 5–10 minutes
Step 3: draft, revise
 • 20–25 minutes
Steps 4 & 5: edit, publish
 • 10–15 minutes

SELF-CHECK

Think about your writing skills. Check (✔) the answers that are true.

1. I understand….
   - ❏ food words.
   - ❏ action verbs.
   - ❏ celebration words.
   - ❏ months and ordinal numbers.
   - ❏ countries and nationalities.

2. I can correctly use…
   - ❏ the imperative form.
   - ❏ count and noncount nouns.
   - ❏ *wh-* questions and answers.
   - ❏ prepositional phrases.
   - ❏ adverbs of frequency.

3. I can correctly use…
   - ❏ a period.
   - ❏ a question mark.
   - ❏ an exclamation point.

4. I can combine sentences…
   - ❏ with signal words.
   - ❏ with connecting words.

5. I can organize my writing by…
   - ❏ time.
   - ❏ importance.

6. I can write to…
   - ❏ explain a procedure.
   - ❏ give information about an event.

Unit 5

Persuade Your Classmates

UNIT OBJECTIVES

Writing
persuasive writing

Organization
main idea and details

Writing Strategies
writing a good paragraph

Vocabulary
things in a neighborhood
sensory adjectives

Grammar
there is/there are
quantity adjectives
the modal *should* for suggestions

Technology
finding maps online

OAK STREET PARK

http://www.eaton*sch

Field Trip Suggestions

(1) The Museum Is Great!
Jake Bye

We should visit the Arlington Museum.

(2) Everybody Loves the Park!

(3) The Nolan Center is Fun!

Admit One

READING

A **Discuss. Work with a partner to answer the questions. Look at the pictures on page 55 for ideas. Compare your answers with another pair.**

1. Where's a popular place in your neighborhood? _____

2. Who goes there? _____

3. What do people do there? _____

4. How do people get there? _____

5. When is a good time to go there? Why? _____

6. Why do people like the place? _____

B **Read. Read the passage about Francisco's neighborhood.**

My Neighborhood
Francisco Garcia

There are many enjoyable things to do in my neighborhood. There's a huge, beautiful park near my apartment. There are many trees in the park. Some trees are tall, and some trees are short. There are many yellow and red flowers in the park, too. They smell very fragrant. There's a lot of thick, green grass in the park, too. The air is fresh and clean. You should go to Oak Street Park on a hot, sunny day.

There is a bright, cheerful mall next to the park. There are twenty-four stores in the mall. There are some expensive stores. Many stores are inexpensive. The bookstore sells books and magazines from around the world. It is usually quiet. The music store sells a lot of popular CDs. It is often loud. There's a movie theater in the mall, too. It is usually crowded on weekends. There are a few restaurants in the mall, as well. Ming's is a great Chinese restaurant. The beef with vegetables at Ming's is delicious. It tastes very spicy and sweet. You should try a little Chinese tea. It's very good.

There are many nice people in my neighborhood. Some people are young, and some people are old. Some people are busy, but some people are not busy. My neighbors are very friendly and helpful. They always smile and say hello. You should meet them sometime.

Learn new words. Write them in your personal dictionary.

C **Write captions. Write a sentence for each picture on page 55. Use sentences from the reading.**

1. There's a huge, beautiful park near my apartment.

2. _____
   _____

3. _____
   _____

4. _____
   _____

5. _____
   _____

6. _____
   _____

7. _____
   _____

8. _____
   _____

9. _____
   _____

10. _____
    _____

11. _____
    _____

12. _____
    _____

VOCABULARY

A **Complete the sentences with words from the box.**

~~neighborhood~~	mall	bookstore	neighbors
music store	grass	movie theater	restaurant
air	park	trees	flowers

1. Francisco's _____neighborhood_____ has many fun things to do.

2. Francisco has a very big _____ near his apartment.

3. The park has many tall and short _____.

4. The _____ in the park are yellow and red.

5. In the park, the _____ is thick and green.

6. The _____ in the park smells fresh and clean.

7. There are twenty-four stores in the _____ near Francisco's home.

8. There are books and magazines from around the world in the _____.

9. The _____ has a lot of popular CDs.

10. The _____ is crowded on weekends.

11. Ming's is a Chinese _____.

12. Francisco has friendly and helpful _____.

B **What do these sensory adjectives describe in the reading on page 54? Write the words in the correct columns.**

Remember!

Sensory adjectives describe how things smell, feel, taste, sound, and look. Add a comma (,) or the word *and* between adjectives.

There is a **huge, beautiful** park near my apartment.
The air is **fresh** and **clean**, too.

quiet	loud	delicious	spicy	huge	beautiful
yellow	red	thick	green	~~fresh~~	clean
tall	short	sweet	hot	fragrant	bright

How does it…				
look?	sound?	feel?	taste?	smell?
				fresh

56 **Step-by-Step Writing** Book 1

C Rewrite the sentences. Replace the underlined words and phrases with synonyms.

bright	huge	beautiful	delicious
~~enjoyable~~	fragrant	friendly	

Remember!

Synonyms have the same (or close to the same) meaning. Use synonyms to make your writing more interesting. Use a thesaurus to find synonyms.
near = close to, by
very good = great, excellent

1. There are many <u>fun</u> things to do in my neighborhood.
   <u>There are many enjoyable things to do in my neighborhood.</u>
2. There's a <u>really</u> big park in my neighborhood. ——————
3. The flowers are very <u>sweet-smelling</u>. ——————
4. My room is red and yellow. It's really <u>colorful</u>. ——————
5. Mr. Chang is a <u>nice</u> man. ——————
6. My sister is <u>pretty</u>. ——————
7. This salad is <u>very good</u>. ——————

GRAMMAR

➤ Learn more in the Grammar Reference, pages 131–141.

Statements with *There is* / *There are*

	Affirmative	Negative
Singular	**There is** a mall next to the park.	**There is no** mall across from the park. **There isn't a** mall across from the park.
Plural	**There are** stores in the mall.	**There are no** stores in the park. **There aren't any** stores in the park.
Noncount Nouns	**There is** grass in the park.	**There is no** grass in the mall. **There isn't any** grass in the mall.

Contractions

There's not = There's no = There isn't

A Write five sentences from the reading on page 54 that use *there is, there's,* or *there are.*

1. <u>There are many enjoyable things to do in my neighborhood.</u>
2. ——————
3. ——————
4. ——————
5. ——————

B These statements are incorrect. Write negative statements. Then add correct information.

1. There are restaurants in the park. <u>There are no restaurants in the park. There are . . .</u>
2. There is an ugly mall next to the park. ——————
3. There are twenty-five stores in the mall. ——————
4. There is an unpopular movie theater in Francisco's neighborhood. ——————

Quantity Adjectives

	Large amounts	Small amounts
Plural count nouns	There are **many** trees in the park. There are **a lot of** children. There are **nineteen** magazines.	There are **some** vegetables. There are **a few** restaurants.
Noncount nouns	There is a **lot of** grass in the park.	**Some** old music is very popular. I had **a little** tea.

Put quantity adjectives **before nouns or other adjectives.**

C Rewrite the sentences. Add quantity adjectives from the reading on page 54.

1. There are enjoyable things in Francisco's neighborhood. <u>There are many enjoyable things in Francisco's neighborhood.</u>

2. There are trees in the park. _____

3. There's also thick, green grass. _____

4. There are stores in the mall. _____

5. Stores are inexpensive. _____

6. There are restaurants in the mall as well. _____

7. People in Francisco's neighborhood are busy. _____

Should and Shouldn't for Suggestions

Affirmative	Negative
You **should visit** Francisco's neighborhood. Francisco **should be** quiet in the bookstore. Francisco and Maria **should go** to the movies on Wednesdays. It's not crowded.	You **shouldn't miss** it. He **shouldn't talk** to Maria. They **shouldn't go** to the movies on weekends. It's very crowded.

D Add *should* or *shouldn't* to the sentences to make suggestions.

1. We _____should_____ visit Francisco's neighborhood.

2. You _____ go to the park on a hot, sunny day.

3. They _____ be loud in the bookstore.

4. You _____ taste the beef with vegetables at Ming's.

5. People _____ smile and say hello to their neighbors.

6. You _____ be mean to your neighbors.

ORGANIZATION

Main Idea and Details

Look at the reading on page 54. Complete the chart. Write the topic sentence and two more supporting sentences for each paragraph.

Remember!
A paragraph is a group of sentences about a topic. The topic sentence gives the main idea of the paragraph. Supporting sentences give details or more information about the topic.

Topic Sentence	Supporting Sentences
There are many enjoyable things to do in my neighborhood.	There's a huge, beautiful park near my apartment. There are many trees in the park. _____ _____
_____ _____ _____	There are twenty-four stores in the mall. _____ _____
_____ _____ _____	Some people are young, and some people are old. _____ _____

WRITING STRATEGIES

Writing a Good Paragraph

This paragraph is incorrect. Study the *Remember* box. Rewrite the paragraph correctly. Indent the first line. Put the topic sentence at the beginning. Delete one sentence that does not connect to the topic sentence.

Remember!
The first line of a paragraph is always indented. The topic sentence of a paragraph is usually at the beginning. Paragraphs usually have three or more sentences. All the sentences in a good paragraph connect to the topic sentence.

My School Is Great

There are many nice, big classrooms. It is clean and bright. I study English in the park. I like my school a lot. It's a good place to study. The teachers are very friendly and helpful.

WRITING

Persuasive Writing

Persuasive writing tries to make an audience agree with the writer's opinion. In a persuasive paragraph, the **topic sentence** usually gives the opinion. **Supporting sentences** give facts or reasons to support the opinion. People often use persuasive writing in letters to the editor and Internet discussion boards.

 A **Read.** Read the class suggestions for their field trip.

http://www.eaton*school*news.ed

Eaton School News

What should we do on our field trip?

The Eaton School Weekly Survey

Mrs. Khatibi: Hi, class! It's time to go out and have some fun. We can learn outside of the classroom, too. I need ideas for our field trip next month. This week's survey question is:

We should visit the Arlington Museum. The building is very old and beautiful. There is a huge dinosaur exhibit at the museum right now. The people at the museum are always nice and helpful. Some people think the museum is boring, but it's really interesting.

posted by Jake Bye, April 5   comment

We should go to the Nolan Theater. The theater has a lot of good events. It has interesting plays and great concerts. The theater is huge and beautiful. Student tickets are very inexpensive. I always have fun there. It's my favorite place!

posted by Sam Walters, April 3   comment

We should go to Eaton Park. There are many big, green trees. There are many beautiful flowers, too. It's very quiet and peaceful. It's a terrific place to go on a nice day.

posted by Michelle Ruiz, April 5   comment

Learn new words. Write them in your personal dictionary.

 B **Write paragraphs.** Write a paragraph for each picture on page 61. Use paragraphs from the Web page.

Persuasive Paragraphs

http://www.eaton*school*news.ed

Field Trip Suggestions

(1) The Museum Is Great!

Jake Bye

We should visit the Arlington Museum.

(2) Everybody Loves the Park!

(3) The Nolan Center is Fun!

STEP–BY–STEP WRITING

Purpose: Persuade Your Classmates

WRITING PROMPT

Your class has a field trip next month. Write a persuasive paragraph. Suggest where the class should go. Write your opinion in the topic sentence. Write reasons for your opinion in three or more supporting sentences. Use interesting information to persuade your classmates.

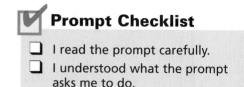

Prompt Checklist

- ❑ I read the prompt carefully.
- ❑ I understood what the prompt asks me to do.

STEP 1 Pre-write

Look at Jake's idea cluster. Make an idea cluster for your suggestion. Write the place in the middle circle. Then add details to support your idea in the circles around it.

Jake's Idea Cluster

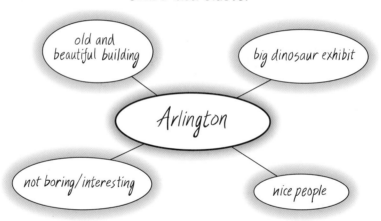

STEP 2 Organize

Look at Jake's paragraph organizer. Copy the organizer into your notebook or make one on a computer. Make an organizer with the main idea and supporting sentences for your persuasive paragraph.

Jake's Paragraph Organizer

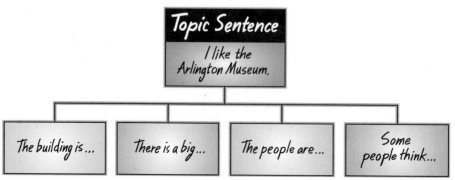

STEP 3 Draft and Revise

A **Practice. Look at Jake's first draft. How can he improve it? Answer the questions.**

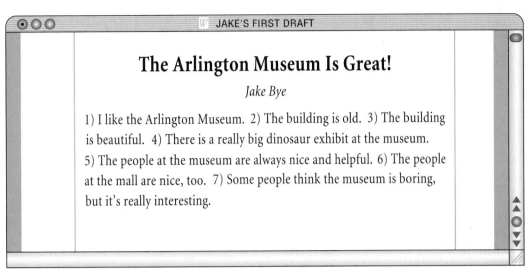

JAKE'S FIRST DRAFT

The Arlington Museum Is Great!

Jake Bye

1) I like the Arlington Museum. 2) The building is old. 3) The building is beautiful. 4) There is a really big dinosaur exhibit at the museum. 5) The people at the museum are always nice and helpful. 6) The people at the mall are nice, too. 7) Some people think the museum is boring, but it's really interesting.

1. What is a more persuasive sentence for sentence 1?

   A I really like the Arlington Museum.
   B You should like the Arlington Museum.
   Ⓒ We should visit the Arlington Museum.
   D I go to the Arlington Museum.

2. What is the best way to combine sentence 2 and sentence 3?

   A The building is old, beautiful.
   B The old building is beautiful.
   C The building is old and beautiful.
   D The building is old and the building is beautiful.

3. What is a more descriptive way to say "really big" in sentence 4?

   A nice
   B huge
   C thick
   D fresh

4. What sentence is NOT a good supporting sentence?

   A Sentence 4
   B Sentence 5
   C Sentence 6
   D Sentence 7

B **Draft. Write a first draft of your persuasive paragraph. Use your notes from Steps 1 and 2.**

C **Revise. Read your first draft. How can you improve it? Look at the revision checklist. Revise your writing.**

✓ Revision Checklist

❑ I gave my opinion in the topic sentence.

❑ I gave reasons for my opinion in supporting sentences.

❑ I included interesting information and adjectives.

STEP 4 Edit

A **Practice.** Look at the sentences. Choose the best substitute for the underlined words. If the sentence is correct, choose "Make no change."

1. The air smells really <u>young</u> in the park.

   A bright
   B quiet
   Ⓒ fresh
   D Make no change.

2. <u>There are many</u> store in my neighborhood.

   A There are a lot of
   B There is many
   C There is one
   D Make no change.

3. <u>Are there any parks</u> near your house?

   A Are there a parks
   B Is there any parks

   C Are there any park
   D Make no change.

4. <u>You should going there</u>. It's nice.

   A You shouldn't go there.
   B You should go there.
   C You should not go there.
   D Make no change.

5. Tim is my new <u>naybor</u>.

   A neighbor
   B nieghbor
   C neghbor
   D Make no change.

B **Edit.** Reread your draft from Step 3. Look at the editing checklist. Edit your writing.

C **Peer Edit.** Exchange drafts with a partner. Tell your partner what you like about the draft. Look at the editing checklist. Tell your partner how to improve the draft.

✔ Editing Checklist

| my |
| me partner |
| ❑ ❑ used sensory and quantity adjectives correctly |
| ❑ ❑ used *There is/There are* correctly |
| ❑ ❑ used *should* for suggestions correctly |
| ❑ ❑ used correct spelling, punctuation, and capitalization |

STEP 5 Publish

Write your persuasive paragraph in your notebook, or on a computer. Look at the field trip suggestions on pages 60 and 61 for ideas. Remember to include your name and a title. Present your persuasive paragraph to the class. What are the most popular suggestions?

TECHNOLOGY

Finding Maps Online

There are many maps on the Internet. There are maps of the world, countries, cities, and even of your neighborhood.

 Use **keyword searches** to find maps of a country, a city, and a neighborhood. **Print** or **download** the three maps if you can. Remember to cite the Internet source for each map.

Unit 6

Describe a Favorite Place

UNIT OBJECTIVES

Writing
descriptive writing

Organization
general to specific

Writing Conventions
spelling

Vocabulary
descriptive adjectives
location phrases
activities

Grammar
present continuous
object pronouns
adverbs

Technology
comparing online resources

READING

 A **Discuss.** Close your eyes and imagine you are in a park on a beautiful day. Answer the questions. Describe the park to your partner. Use sensory details.

1. Where are you? _____

2. What do you see? _____

3. What do you smell? _____

4. What do you hear? _____

5. What do you feel? _____

B **Read.** Read Francisco's description of Oak Street Park.

A Day in Oak Street Park
Francisco Garcia

Learn new words. Write them in your personal dictionary.

There are many interesting places in my neighborhood. One place is Oak Street Park. I am at Oak Street Park right now. It's my favorite place. It's 1:00 on Saturday afternoon. I am sitting on a bench and writing in my journal. Today is a beautiful day. It's really sunny and hot. The sky is clear and bright. The air smells fresh and sweet.

The park is very crowded. Some people are young, and some people are old. Some people are tall, and some are short. Some people have long, straight hair. Some people have short, curly hair. One old man has no hair! He is standing in front of the park gate. A tall woman is standing beside him. She has blonde hair and blue eyes. They are talking and laughing loudly.

There are a lot of things happening around me. Many people are exercising. They're walking quickly or riding their bikes. There is a food stand to the right of the entrance. A few people are eating lunch next to it. There is a handsome man to the left of the entrance. He is painting a picture very carefully. Across from me, a young girl is playing under a tree. Her brother is playing with her, too. They're running and jumping happily. Their mother is sitting behind them. She is watching them quietly. Everyone is having fun.

 C **Write captions.** Write a sentence for each picture on page 67. Use sentences from the reading.

1. I'm at Oak Street Park
   right now.

2. _____

3. _____

4. _____

5. _____

6. _____

7. _____

8. _____

9. _____

10. _____

VOCABULARY

A Complete the chart with the opposite adjectives from the reading on page 66. Write the sentences in your notebook.

from the reading on page 66

Opposites Chart	
unattractive	1. handsome
tall	2.
long, straight	3.
young	4.

Remember!
You can use descriptive adjectives to add details. They can go before nouns or after the verb *be*.

The **tall** woman is in the park.
She is **tall**.

Some people have **short, curly** hair.
Their hair is **short** and **curly**.

1. There is a handsome man to the left of the entrance.

2.

B Write the correct location phrases for each sentence. Use information from the reading and pictures on pages 66 and 67.

Use information from the reading and pictures on pages 66 and 67.

Remember!
Location phrases tell where something is located.

I'm **in** my favorite place.
I'm **at** Oak Street Park.

next to	in front of	~~on~~	across from
beside	to the right of	under	behind

1. Francisco is _____ on _____ a bench.

2. An older man is _____ the park gate.

3. A tall woman is _____ him.

4. There is a food stand _____ the entrance.

5. A few people are _____ the food stand.

6. A young girl is _____ Francisco.

7. The girl is _____ a tree.

8. The children's mother is _____ them.

C Complete the sentences about the Garcia family. Use the correct form of the verb.

run	jump	talk	~~exercise~~
watch	laugh	ride	paint

1. Francisco usually _____exercises_____ at the gym in the morning.

2. Mr. Garcia often _____ TV in the evening.

3. Sometimes he _____ if a program is funny.

4. In her free time, Mrs. Garcia _____ beautiful pictures.

5. She often _____ with her friends on the telephone, too.

6. Maria often _____ in the park for exercise. She's really fast.

7. She also sometimes _____ rope.

8. Francisco and Maria never _____ their bikes to school. Their school is very close.

GRAMMAR

➤ Learn more in the Grammar Reference, pages 131-141.

A Imagine it is Saturday afternoon. What are the people doing right now? Change the sentences to the present continuous tense.

Present Tenses	
Simple Present Tense	**Present Continuous Tense**
Francisco **writes** in his journal every day.	Francisco **is writing** in his journal right now.
People **exercise** in the park on Saturdays.	Some people **are exercising** right now.

The **present continuous tense** tells what is happening right now.

1. Maria and her friends play soccer every Saturday afternoon.
   Maria and her friends are playing soccer right now.

2. Mrs. Garcia eats lunch with her friends every Saturday afternoon.

   _____

3. Francisco's classmates exercise every Saturday afternoon.

   _____

4. Mr. and Mrs. Garcia watch a movie every Saturday afternoon.

   _____

5. Francisco relaxes in the park every Saturday afternoon.

   _____

B Rewrite each sentence. Change the underlined words to object pronouns.

Object Pronouns	
Noun	**Object Pronoun**
A tall woman is talking to **the man**. The girl's brother is playing with **the girl**. The mother is watching **her children**. People are eating lunch next to **a food stand**.	A tall woman is talking to **him**. The girl's brother is playing with **her**. The mother is watching **them**. People are eating lunch next to **it**.

1. Francisco is writing in <u>his journal</u>. _____ *Francisco is writing in it.* _____

2. There is a food stand to the right of <u>the entrance</u>. _____

3. The boy's sister is playing with <u>the boy</u>. _____

4. An older man is talking to <u>a tall woman</u>. _____

5. Francisco is watching <u>the brother and sister</u>. _____

6. The children are playing across from <u>Francisco</u>. _____

C The sentences below are not true. Rewrite the sentences. Use the correct adverb from the passage on page 66.

Adverbs answer the question "How?" They give details about verbs, adjectives, and other adverbs. Many adverbs end in *-ly*. *Really* and *very* are also adverbs.

Adverbs		
Question	**Description**	**Purpose**
How is the mother watching her children?	She's watching them **quietly**.	gives details about the verb *watch*
How hot is it?	It's **really** hot.	gives details about the adjective *hot*
How carefully is the man painting?	The man is painting **very carefully**.	gives details about the adverb *carefully*

1. It's *not* sunny. _____ *It's really sunny.* _____

2. People in the park are walking *slowly*. _____

3. A man is painting very *carelessly*. _____

4. An older man and a tall woman are talking and laughing *quietly*. _____

5. A brother and sister are playing *sadly* in the park. _____

ORGANIZATION

General to Specific

Number the sentences in order from general to specific. Then, write a paragraph. Write the sentences in the correct order.

Remember!
You can start with general information and then give specific details. In the reading on page 66, Francisco first describes the general setting (place and time) and tells what he is doing. Then he adds specific details about the characters (people). Then he describes the action (what is happening).

Group 1

_____ I'm staying home and watching a movie.

___1___ It's a cold, wet Saturday in Washington, D.C.

_____ They are singing and dancing.

_____ There are many people in the movie.

Group 2

_____ Some people are playing football. Some people are relaxing.

_____ Carson Beach is very popular. It has water sports, a picnic area, and food stands.

_____ Carson City is very beautiful in the summer. It is a great place for a vacation.

_____ The beach is always very crowded. Many people are at Carson Beach right now.

It's a cold, wet Saturday...

WRITING CONVENTIONS

Spelling

The words in the boxes are not spelled correctly. Rewrite the description. Correct the misspelled words.

Remember!
Many words are difficult to spell. Use a dictionary or spell check. See page 143 for a list of commonly misspelled words.

a lot

There are alot of things happening around me. Many people are exersising. There walking quickly or riding their bikes. There is a food stand to the rihgt of the entrance. A few people are eating lunch next to it. There is a handsome man to the left of the entrance. He is painting a picture very carfully. Acros from me, a young girl is playing under a tree. Her brother is playing with her, to. They're runing and jumping happily. Thier mother is sitting behind them. She is watching them quitly. Everyone is haveing fun.

There are a lot of things ...

Descriptive Writing

Descriptive writing tells how something looks, tastes, smells, sounds, feels, or makes a person feel. A detailed description makes the setting, characters, and action seem real. Stories and journal entries often use descriptive writing.

A **Read.** Read the journal descriptions of these students' favorite places.

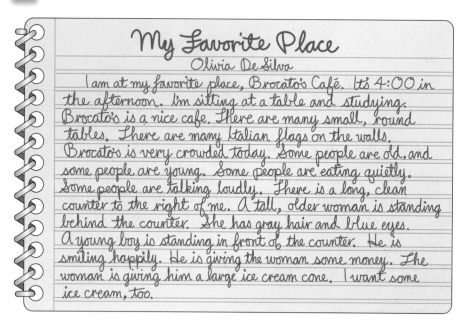

My Favorite Place
Olivia De Silva

I am at my favorite place, Brocato's Café. It's 4:00 in the afternoon. I'm sitting at a table and studying. Brocato's is a nice cafe. There are many small, round tables. There are many Italian flags on the walls. Brocato's is very crowded today. Some people are old, and some people are young. Some people are eating quietly. Some people are talking loudly. There is a long, clean counter to the right of me. A tall, older woman is standing behind the counter. She has gray hair and blue eyes. A young boy is standing in front of the counter. He is smiling happily. He is giving the woman some money. The woman is giving him a large ice cream cone. I want some ice cream, too.

Learn new words. Write them in your personal dictionary.

Sports World Is My Favorite Place
Kim Lawden

My friend Kristi and I are relaxing at Sports World. It's 1:00 on Sunday. Sports World is a popular recreation center in my neighborhood. There's a huge basketball court next to the entrance. It is clean and shiny. There are three tennis courts to the left of it. They are big and bright. There is a batting cage across from the tennis courts. It's really noisy. There are a lot of people at Sports World. Many people are exercising. Several tall boys are playing basketball. They are running and jumping. Four older ladies are playing tennis. They are laughing loudly. My classmate is hitting baseballs. He is short. He has black hair and brown eyes. Maybe I should say hello.

B **Write paragraphs.** Look at the pictures on page 73. Write the correct paragraph under each picture.

Descriptive Paragraphs

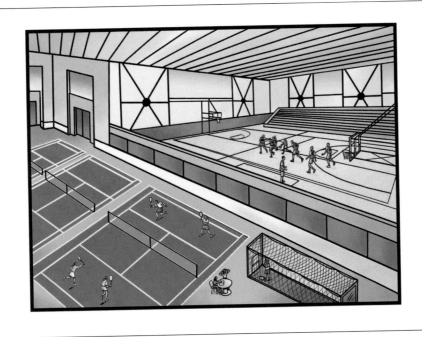

STEP–BY–STEP WRITING

Purpose: Describe a Favorite Place

WRITING PROMPT

Imagine you are in a favorite place. Write a journal entry. First, give general information about the place, time, and what you are doing. Then, give more specific information about the place and the people around you. Finally, give details about something that is happening near you.

✔ Prompt Checklist

- ☐ I read the prompt carefully.
- ☐ I understood what the prompt asks me to do.

STEP 1 Pre-write

Look at Olivia's notes. Imagine you are in a favorite place. Write notes about your favorite place in your notebook. Remember to include general information, specific information, and details.

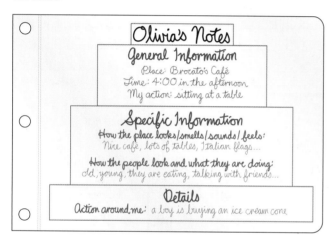

Olivia's Notes

General Information
Place: Brocato's Café
Time: 4:00 in the afternoon
My action: sitting at a table

Specific Information
How the place looks/smells/sounds/feels:
Nice café, lots of tables, Italian flags...
How the people look and what they are doing:
old, young, they are eating, talking with friends...

Details
Action around me: a boy is buying an ice cream cone

STEP 2 Organize

Look at Olivia's organizer. Organize your ideas. Copy the chart in your notebook or make one on a computer. Complete the chart with notes for your description.

Olivia's Organizer

Topic Sentence	I am in my favorite place, Brocato's Café.
General Information	It's 4:00 in the afternoon. I'm sitting...
Specific Information	Brocato's is a nice café. There are a lot of... Some people are old. Some people are...
Details	A young boy is buying...

STEP 3 Draft and Revise

A **Practice. Look at Olivia's first draft. How can she improve it? Answer the questions.**

OLIVIA'S FIRST DRAFT

1) I am in my favorite place, Brocato's Café. 2) It's about 4:00 in the afternoon. 3) I'm sitting at a table. 4) I'm studying. 5) Brocato's is a nice café. 6) There are small tables in the café. 7) There are Italian flags on the walls. 8) Brocato's is very crowded today. 9) Some people are old, and some people are young. 10) People are eating ice cream and talking. 11) There is a counter to the right of me. 12) A tall, older woman is standing behind the counter. 13) A boy is standing in front of the counter. 14) The boy is smiling happily. 15) The boy is giving the woman some money. 16) The woman is giving the boy a large ice cream cone. I want some ice cream, too.

---

1. What is the best way to combine sentences 3 and 4?

   A I'm sitting at a table but studying.
   B I'm sitting at a table or studying.
   Ⓒ I'm sitting at a table and studying.
   D I'm at a table sitting studying.

2. What's the best way to add more details to sentence 10?

   A Some people are quiet and some people are loud.
   B Some people are eating. Some people are talking.
   C Some people are eating quietly. Some people are talking loudly.
   D Some people are eating quietly. Some people talk.

3. Where should Olivia add this descriptive sentence?

   | She has gray hair and blue eyes. |

   A after Sentence 10
   B after Sentence 11
   C after Sentence 12
   D after Sentence 13

4. What is another word for "the boy" in sentence 16?

   A him
   B his
   C her
   D he

B **Draft. Write a first draft of your descriptive paragraph. Use your notes from Steps 1 and 2.**

C **Revise. Read your first draft. How can you improve it? Look at the revision checklist. Revise your writing.**

✔ Revision Checklist

❑ I gave general information about the setting and my action.
❑ I gave specific information about the place and the people.
❑ I gave details about something happening near me.
❑ I included descriptive adjectives and adverbs.

Step 4 Edit

A **Practice.** Look at the sentences. Choose the best word or phrase to complete each sentence.

1. There _____ a tall, older woman in the park.

   Ⓐ is
   B has
   C have
   D are

2. A woman is standing _____ me.

   A across
   B right
   C behind
   D next

3. Mary _____ right now.

   A is paint a picture
   B paints a picture

   C painting a picture
   D isn't painting a picture

4. Alex is talking to _____ now.

   A his
   B she
   C their
   D them

5. Kerry is walking _____.

   A very
   B cheerful
   C careful
   D slowly

B **Edit.** Reread your draft from Step 3. Look at the editing checklist. Edit your writing.

C **Peer Edit.** Exchange drafts with a partner. Tell your partner what you like about the draft. Look at the editing checklist. Tell your partner how to improve the draft.

STEP 5 Publish

Write your descriptive paragraph in your notebook or on a computer. Look at the models on pages 72 and 73 for ideas. Remember to include your name and a title. Present your descriptive paragraph to the class. Do your classmates feel like they are in your favorite place with you?

✔ Editing Checklist

me	my partner	
☐	☐	used descriptive adjectives, adverbs, and location words correctly
☐	☐	used the present continuous tense and object pronouns correctly
☐	☐	used correct spelling, punctuation, and capitalization

TECHNOLOGY

Comparing Online Resources

Do an Internet keyword search for *online ESL dictionary*. Look up the word *describe* on three dictionary Web sites. Highlight the first definition in each dictionary. Use Ctrl+C or Command+C to copy the text. Open a new word processing document. Use Ctrl+V or Command+V to paste the definition. Remember to cite each source. Are all three dictionary definitions the same? Present your information to the class.

GROUP WRITING

Work in a group to write about one of these topics.

1. Choose your subject.
2. Study the information.
3. Write a topic sentence.
4. Add supporting information.
5. Revise and edit the writing with your group.
6. Present your group's writing to the class.

Topic 1

Write a persuasive paragraph to Heinle Publishing. Make suggestions and support your reasons.

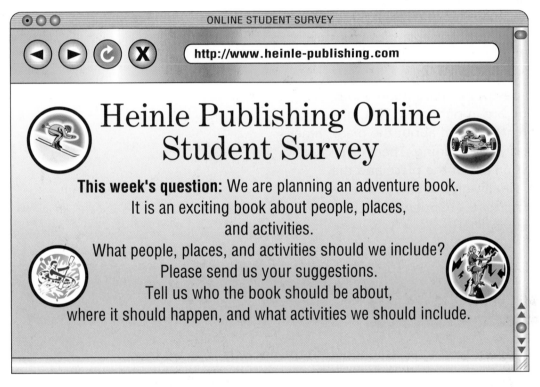

ONLINE STUDENT SURVEY

http://www.heinle-publishing.com

Heinle Publishing Online Student Survey

This week's question: We are planning an adventure book.
It is an exciting book about people, places,
and activities.
What people, places, and activities should we include?
Please send us your suggestions.
Tell us who the book should be about,
where it should happen, and what activities we should include.

Topic 2

Write a descriptive paragraph about this illustration. Describe the place and tell what is happening.

TIMED WRITING

Choose one writing prompt. Complete the writing task in 45 minutes.

WRITING PROMPT 1

You are planning a trip with a group of friends. Write a persuasive message to the group. Suggest where you think you should go. Write your opinion in the topic sentence. Write reasons for your opinion in three or more supporting sentences. Use interesting information and adjectives to persuade the group.

WRITING PROMPT 2

Write a descriptive paragraph about the room you are in right now. First, give general information about the place, time, and what you are doing. Then, give specific information about the place and the people. Finally, give details about something that is happening.

Test Tip

Stay on topic! Reread your topic sentence as you write your paragraph. All the supporting sentences should connect to the topic sentence.

SELF-CHECK

Think about your writing skills. Check (✔) the answers that are true.

1. I understand…
   - ❏ neighborhood words.
   - ❏ sensory adjectives.
   - ❏ descriptive adjectives.
   - ❏ location phrases.
   - ❏ activity words.

2. I can correctly use…
   - ❏ there is/there are.
   - ❏ quantity adjectives.
   - ❏ the modal *should* for suggestions.
   - ❏ the present continuous tense.
   - ❏ object pronouns.
   - ❏ adverbs.

3. I can correctly…
   - ❏ indent my paragraphs.
   - ❏ write a topic sentence.
   - ❏ write supporting sentences.
   - ❏ fix spelling errors in a paragraph.

4. I can organize my writing by …
   - ❏ main idea and details.
   - ❏ general to specific.

5. I can write to…
   - ❏ persuade.
   - ❏ describe a place.

Unit 7

Write a Message to a Friend

UNIT OBJECTIVES

Writing
writing a friendly letter or e-mail

Organization
parts of a letter

Writing Conventions
mailing addresses

Vocabulary
days of the week
free-time activities
time expressions
feelings and moods

Grammar
simple past tense with regular
 verbs
simple past tense with *be* and
 have

Technology
sending an electronic message

april 12, 2008
(heading)

(greeting)

(body)

(closing)

Tom
(signature)

A **Discuss.** What do you do on weekends? Complete the survey with a partner. Then, share your information with the class.

How often do you...

	Often	Sometimes	Never
play sports?			
study?			
talk with your friends?			
watch TV?			
exercise?			

B **Read.** Read Francisco's letter to his cousin, Pedro.

Learn new words. Write them in your personal dictionary.

March 7, 2008

Dear Pedro,

My computer isn't working, so I'm writing you a letter. How are you? I'm fine. Everything here in L.A. is great. I'm very happy. School is going well. I have a lot of classes this year. I play sports in my free time, too. I'm really busy.

Last weekend was fun. On Saturday, I had a basketball game at 7:00 in the morning. I was very sleepy. Maria didn't play because she was sick. After the game, I shopped for groceries with my mom and dad. We finally had lunch at noon. I was really hungry. After that, I was a little bored, but my friend Rick called me. We walked to the mall. We shopped until about 6:00 in the evening. On Saturday night, I played games and watched TV with my family. We had fun. On Sunday, we weren't busy. We stayed home because we didn't have any plans. In the morning, I cleaned my room for about an hour. Then, Maria and I studied from about 1:00 p.m. to 3:00 p.m. After that, I worked out and Maria practiced the guitar. On Sunday evening, I relaxed because I was tired.

How about you? Did you have a good weekend? What did you do? Tell Aunt Marina and Uncle Umberto hello for me. Write soon!

Your cousin,
Francisco

C **Write captions.** Write a sentence under each picture on page 81. Use sentences from Francisco's letter.

1. My computer isn't working, so I'm writing you a letter.

2. _____

3. _____

4. _____

5. _____

6. _____

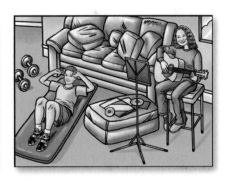

7. _____

8. _____

9. _____

VOCABULARY

A Complete Francisco's weekly schedule with the days of the week.

Wednesday
~~Sunday~~
Thursday
Monday
Saturday
Tuesday
Friday

Francisco's Schedule

1. Sunday	2.	3.	4.	5.	6.	7.
			morning			
clean my room	6:00 a.m. to 7:00 a.m. – work out 7:30 a.m. to 2:30 p.m. – school	7:30 a.m. to 2:30 p.m. – school	6:00 a.m. to 7:00 a.m. – work out 7:30 a.m. to 2:30 p.m. – school	7:30 a.m. to 2:30 p.m. – school	6:00 a.m. to 7:00 a.m. – work out 7:30 a.m. to 2:30 p.m. – school	7:00 a.m. to 9:00 a.m. – play basketball 10:30 a.m. to 12:00 p.m. – shop for groceries
			afternoon			
	2:30 p.m. to 3:30 p.m. – study with math group 4:00 p.m. to 6:00 p.m. – study	4:00 p.m. to 6:00 p.m. – study	4:00 p.m. to 6:00 p.m. – study	4:00 p.m. to 6:00 p.m. – study	4:00 p.m. to 6:00 p.m. – study	
			evening			
stay home and relax		6:30 p.m. to 8:00 p.m. – practice guitar with Maria	7:00 p.m. – call Grandma Garcia in San Diego	6:30 p.m. to 8:00 p.m. – practice guitar with Maria		

B Read the sentences. What is Francisco doing at these times? Look at Francisco's schedule in Exercise A. Write sentences. Use the present continuous tense.

1. It's 3:15 on Monday afternoon. _He's studying with his math group._

2. It's 7:00 on Thursday evening. _____

3. It's 6:30 on Friday morning. _____

4. It's 8:45 on Saturday morning. _____

5. It's 10:45 on Sunday morning. _____

6. It's 7:00 on Wednesday evening. _____

C Answer the questions. Use information from Francisco's schedule in Exercise A. Use the prepositions in parentheses.

Remember!
Time expressions tell when something happens or how long something lasts.
| When | in the morning | on Saturday | at 12:00 p.m./at noon |
| How long | for two hours | from 3:00 to 5:00 | |

1. How long does Francisco play basketball on Saturday? (for) _He plays basketball for two hours._

2. What time does Francisco call Grandma Garcia? (at) _____

3. What day does Francisco clean his room? (on) _____

4. When does Francisco work out? (in) _____

5. How long does Francisco practice the guitar on Tuesdays and Thursdays? (from . . . to)

_____

D These sentences are not true. Rewrite the sentences. Use the correct adjectives from Francisco's letter on page 80.

1. Francisco is *sad* in Los Angeles. <u>Francisco is happy in Los Angeles.</u>

2. Francisco was *wide awake* on Saturday morning. _____

3. Maria didn't play basketball because she was *healthy*. _____

4. Francisco was *full* at noon. _____

5. Francisco was *busy* after lunch. _____

6. Francisco was *full of energy* on Sunday evening. _____

GRAMMAR   ➤ Learn more in the Grammar Reference, pages 131–141.

A Write correct sentences. Use information from the letter on page 80. Use the past tense of the verb in parentheses. Use *didn't* for negative statements.

Simple Past Tense of Regular Verbs		
Verb	**Affirmative Statements**	**Negative Statements**
play **study**	Francisco **played** basketball on Saturday. Maria and Francisco **studied** on Sunday afternoon.	Maria **didn't play** basketball. They **didn't study** on Saturday night.

Add *-ed* or *-d* to form the simple past tense of most regular verbs. There are some exceptions:

study → stud**ied**   shop → shop**ped**

1. Maria (play) basketball on Saturday morning. <u>Maria didn't play basketball on Saturday morning.</u>

2. Francisco's friend Rick (call) him on Saturday afternoon. _____
_____

3. Francisco and Rick (walk) to the mall in the morning. _____

4. Maria and Francisco (watch TV) on Saturday night. _____

5. On Sunday, Maria and Francisco (stay home) all day. _____

6. On Sunday morning, Francisco (clean) his room for three hours. _____

7. On Sunday, Francisco (work out) and Maria (practice) the guitar. _____

8. On Sunday evening, Francisco (relax). _____

B Write complete sentences. Use information from the letter on page 80. Change *be* or *have* to the past tense. Add the correct preposition to the time expressions.

	Simple Past Tense with *be* and *have*	
Verb	Affirmative Statements	Negative Statements
be	Francisco **was** tired on Sunday night. Francisco and his parents **were** busy on Saturday morning.	He **wasn't** tired on Saturday night. They **weren't** busy on Saturday night.
have	Francisco **had** a basketball game on Saturday morning. Francisco and his family **had** plans on Saturday.	He **didn't have** a game on Sunday morning. They **didn't have** plans on Sunday.

1. Francisco / has / a basketball game / 7:00 a.m.

   Francisco had a basketball game at 7:00 a.m.

2. Maria / is / sick / Saturday morning

   _____

3. Francisco / has lunch / noon

   _____

4. Saturday afternoon / Francisco / is / bored

   _____

5. Saturday night / Francisco and his family / have / fun

   _____

7. Sunday / Francisco and Maria / are not / busy

   _____

8. Sunday / the Garcia family / do not have / any plans

   _____

C Complete the story summary about Francisco's weekend. Use the correct form of the past tense.

    Francisco (1) __had__ fun last weekend. He (2) _____ basketball on Saturday. He (3) _____ sleepy. Maria (4) _____ home because she (5) _____ sick. After the game, Francisco (6) _____ for groceries. Then, he (7) _____ lunch. After that, he and his friend Rick (8) _____ over to the mall. On Saturday night, Francisco and his family didn't (9) _____ any plans. They (10) _____ games and (11) _____ TV. On Sunday, Maria and Francisco (12) _____ busy. Francisco (13) _____ his room. Then he and Maria (14) _____ from 1:00 to 3:00. On Sunday evening, Francisco (15) _____ tired.

ORGANIZATION

Parts of a Letter

A Look at Francisco's letter on page 80. Find the five parts of his letter.

Look at Francisco's letter on page 80.

> **Remember!**
> There are usually five parts of a letter. The heading gives the date of the letter. The greeting says "hello" to the person you are writing to (the receiver.) The body of the letter is the message. It is in paragraph form. The closing says "good-bye" to the receiver. The signature is the signed name under the closing.

B The letter is incorrect. Read the information and label the parts of the letter. Then, rewrite the letter in the correct order.

<u>closing</u> Your friend,

_____ How are you? I'm great. I'm sitting in the park right now. I'm relaxing with my friends. Last weekend was really exciting. I went to Seattle with my family. We had a really good time. How was your weekend? Did you do anything interesting? Write soon!

_____ November 23, 2008

_____ Dear Rachel,

_____ MARCI HESS

WRITING CONVENTIONS

Mailing Addresses

Label the parts of Francisco's address. Then, write your school's address. Use correct abbreviations.

> **Remember!**
> An address gives the receiver's name and location. The return address gives the writer's information. Put a comma between the street address and apartment number. Put a comma between the city and state. You can use abbreviations. For example:
> Apt. (Apartment)   N. (North)
> CA (California)   St. (Street)

For international addresses, add the country name to the end of the address.

| house / building number | apartment number | street name | ~~receiver name~~ |
| city name | state name | zip code |

receiver name — Francisco Garcia

145 Oak Street, Apt. #9

Los Angeles, CA 90802

West Public School

15 N. Broad . . . .

Writing a Friendly Letter or E-mail

In a friendly letter or e-mail, the author writes an informal message to a friend or family member. These messages often tell how the author is feeling. They can also tell about recent activities or events. The author may also ask the receiver questions, or make simple requests.

  A **Read.** Read Tom's e-mail to a friend.

Learn new words. Write them in your personal dictionary.

From: Tom Botsford (tbotsford@h-net.com)
To: Alicia O'Brien (ao'brien@t-com.net)
Subject: Hi there!
Date: April 12, 2008
Hi Alicia,

Things here in Miami are fine. I'm very busy. I have classes Monday to Friday from 9:00 a.m. to 3:00 p.m. My classes are interesting. I like my teachers, too.

Last weekend was great. On Friday evening, I played soccer with some classmates. On Saturday morning, I listened to music and cleaned my room. Then, I had a big breakfast. I was hungry. After that, I studied from 11:00 a.m. until 1:00 p.m. Then in the afternoon, my friend Marco and I played basketball. On Sunday morning, I just relaxed because I was tired. Then, I called my grandmother on Sunday afternoon. On Sunday night, I played games with my family. We had a great time!

How are you? How is school? Are you busy? Write soon!
See you later!
Tom

 B **Write a letter.** Rewrite Tom's e-mail to Alicia as a friendly letter. Use the format on page 87.

A Friendly Letter

April 12, 2008

(heading)

_____

(greeting)

_____

(body)

_____

(closing)

Tom

(signature)

STEP-BY-STEP WRITING

Purpose: Write a Message to a Friend

WRITING PROMPT

Write a letter or e-mail to a friend or family member. First, tell the person how you are. Then, write about what you did last weekend. Use time expressions to sequence events. Finally, ask questions or make requests.

☑ Prompt Checklist

- ❑ I read the prompt carefully.
- ❑ I understood what the prompt asks me to do.

STEP 1 Pre-write

Look at Tom's cluster map. Think about what you want to say. Copy the cluster map or make one on a computer. Put the main topic in the center. Complete the cluster map with your information.

Tom's Cluster Map

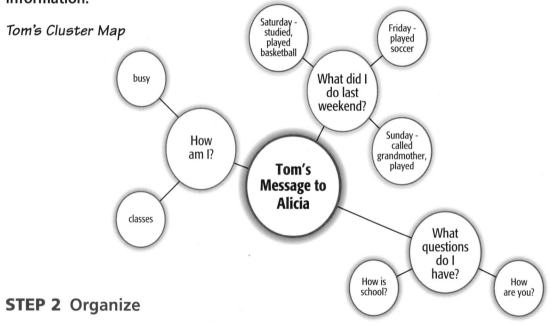

STEP 2 Organize

Look at Tom's message outline. Organize your ideas. Copy the chart in your notebook or make one on a computer. Complete the chart with notes for your message.

Tom's Message Outline	
Greeting	*Dear Alicia,*
Body	**How am I?** *I'm busy. School is good. I have class from …*
	What did I do last weekend? *On Friday, I played …*
	What questions do I have? *How are you? How is school? Are you busy?*
Closing	*Your friend,*

STEP 3 Draft and Revise

A **Practice. Look at Tom's first draft of the body of his message. How can he improve it? Answer the questions.**

TOM'S FIRST DRAFT

1) I have classes Monday to Friday from 9:00 a.m. to 3:00 p.m. 2) My classes are interesting. 3) Things here in Miami are fine. 4) I like my teachers, too.

5) Last weekend was great. 6) On Friday evening, I played soccer with some classmates. 7) On Saturday morning, I listened to music and cleaned my room. 8) Then, I had a big breakfast. 9) I was sleepy. 10) After that, I studied from 11:00 a.m. until 1:00 p.m. 11) Then in the afternoon, I played basketball. 12) My friend Marco played basketball, too. 13) On Sunday morning, I just relaxed because I was tired. 14) Then, I called my grandmother on Sunday afternoon. 15) On Sunday night, I played games with my family. 16) We had a great time.

17) How are you? 18) How was your weekend? 19) Did you have fun? 20) I'm fine. 21) Please write soon!

1. What is a better topic sentence for paragraph 1?
   A Sentence 2
   Ⓑ Sentence 3
   C Sentence 4
   D Make no change.

2. What's the best way to combine sentences 11 and 12?
   A Then in the afternoon, my friend and Marco played basketball.
   B Then in the afternoon, my friend Marco played basketball.
   C Then in the afternoon, my friend Marco and I played basketball.
   D Then in the afternoon, my Marco and I played basketball.

3. What is a better word for "sleepy" in sentence 9?
   A fine
   B bored
   C tired
   D hungry

4. What sentence does not fit in paragraph 3?
   A Sentence 17
   B Sentence 18
   C Sentence 19
   D Sentence 20

B **Draft. Write a first draft of your friendly letter or e-mail. Use your notes from Steps 1 and 2.**

C **Revise. Read your first draft. How can you improve it? Look at the revision checklist. Revise your writing.**

☑ Revision Checklist

- ❑ I told how I am.
- ❑ I wrote about last weekend.
- ❑ I used time expressions to order the events.
- ❑ I asked questions or made requests.

STEP 4 Edit

A **Practice.** Look at the sentences. Choose the best substitute for the underlined words. If the sentence is correct, choose "Make no change."

1. I did my homework <u>to</u> three hours on Sunday.

    A from

    B at

    C for

    D Make no change.

2. My sister practices the guitar <u>in</u> Monday afternoons.

    A on

    B at

    C to

    D Make no change.

3. We <u>watches</u> movies last weekend.

    A are watching

    B watched

    C watch

    D Make no change.

4. Rachel <u>haven't</u> breakfast last Sunday.

    A hadn't

    B didn't have

    C didn't had

    D Make no change.

5. Perry Martin
   4152 Elm St.
   <u>Los Angeles CA 02128</u>

    A Los Angeles, CA 02128

    B Los Angeles CA, 02128

    C Los Angeles C.A. 02128

    D Make no change.

B **Edit.** Reread your draft from Step 3. Look at the editing checklist. Edit your writing.

C **Peer Edit.** Exchange drafts with a partner. Tell your partner what you like about the draft. Look at the editing checklist. Tell your partner how to improve the draft.

✔ Editing Checklist

me	my partner	
☐	☐	used new time, activity, mood, and feeling words correctly
☐	☐	used the simple past tense correctly
☐	☐	used correct spelling, punctuation, and capitalization

STEP 5 Publish

Write your message in friendly letter or e-mail format. For a friendly letter, include all five parts for the letter. Present your letter to the class or mail it to your friend. For e-mails, type your message in e-mail format on a computer. Print a copy or send it to your teacher.

TECHNOLOGY

Sending an Electronic Message

You can send messages on the Internet with e-mail (electronic mail) or e-cards (electronic cards). Do a keyword search for "free e-cards." Click on a hyperlink. Do not click on an advertisement. Follow the site directions to send an e-card to a friend, family member, or teacher.

Unit 8

Invite People to an Event

UNIT OBJECTIVES

Writing
writing a formal letter

Organization
chronological order

Writing Strategies
form, audience, topic, purpose

Vocabulary
event words
time expressions
comparative adjectives

Grammar
future tense with *be going to*
formal requests and invitations

Technology
finding local events

A **Discuss.** Imagine there is a celebration at your school next week. What activities should your school have? Work with a partner. Check (✓) the three activities you like the best. Persuade another pair of students that your suggestions are the best.

❏ go to the park   ❏ have a school dance   ❏ have a talent show
❏ have a costume contest   ❏ plan a tour   ❏ make special food

B **Read.** Read the letter from Francisco's school.

Oak Street School
170 Oak Street
Los Angeles, CA 90007
April 5, 2008

Learn new words. Write them in your personal dictionary.

Mr. and Mrs. Garcia
145 Oak St., Apt. 9
Los Angeles, CA 90007

Dear Mr. and Mrs. Garcia:

It is time for our Fun Time Festival. The festival is going to start Monday, April 12, and end Friday, April 16. This year's celebration is going to be bigger than last year's celebration.

As usual, the school is going to have an exciting event every day. On "Museum Monday," students are going to take a tour of the museum of art. Students should be at the school at 7:45 a.m. They should not be late because the bus is going to leave at 8:00 a.m. For "Dance Tuesday," the school is going to have a salsa dance party. The party is going to start at 4:30 p.m. Students should be on time. On "Wild Wednesday," students should wear wild and crazy hats. The wildest and craziest hat wins a prize. On "Costume Thursday," the school is going to have a costume contest. Students should wear costumes to school. The best costume wins a prize.

The busiest day is going to be "Fun Friday." In the morning, students are not going to have class. They are going to practice before the talent show. After that, the school is going to have a picnic lunch. Finally, the talent show is going to start at 1:00 p.m. It's going to be very exciting.

We would like to invite all family members to the talent show on Friday afternoon. It is going to be very crowded, so please come early. Please reply to Mrs. Percy or me by next Friday if you are going to come. Thank you.

Sincerely,

Alma Rivera

Ms. Alma Rivera, School Principal

C **Write captions.** Write a sentence for each picture on page 93. Use sentences from the reading.

1. The festival is going to start Monday, April 12 and end Friday, April 16.

2. _____
   _____
   _____

3. _____
   _____
   _____

4. _____
   _____
   _____

5. _____
   _____
   _____

6. _____
   _____
   _____

7. _____
   _____
   _____

8. _____
   _____
   _____

VOCABULARY

A Complete Francisco's paragraph about the Fun Time Festival. Use the words in the box.

~~Festival~~	events	tour	contest	party
prize	show	invites	costume	

    The Fun Time (1) <u>Festival</u> is a popular celebration at the Oak Street School. Every year, we have many different (2) _____. Last year, Monday's event was a (3) _____ of the history museum. Then, on Tuesday, there was a hip hop dance (4) _____ at the school. I danced all night! Wednesday was "Crazy Hair Day." There was a (5) _____ for the craziest hair style, but I didn't win. On Thursday, we had a "Movie Magic (6) _____." The person with the most interesting (7) _____ from a movie was the winner. The most exciting event was the talent (8) _____ on Friday morning. Mom and Dad were there, too. Ms. Rivera always (9) _____ students' families. We all had a lot of fun.

B Rewrite the sentences. Use the correct word in parentheses to create the correct time expression. Use information from the letter on page 92.

1. This year's Fun Time Festival is (last/next) week. <u>This year's Fun Time Festival is next week.</u>

2. There are many different events (last/every) year. _____

3. (Last/Next) year's celebration was big. _____

4. Students should not be (late/early) for the museum tour. _____

5. They should come (on time/late) for the dance party. _____

6. (Next/This) year, students should wear wild hats. _____

7. On Friday, students should practice (before/after) the talent show. _____

8. On Friday, parents should come (on time/early) for the talent show. _____

C Rewrite each sentence with the correct form of the adjective. Use information from the reading on page 92.

1. This year's celebration is going to be (big/bigger/ biggest) than last year's celebration.

2. The school is going to have an (exciting/more exciting/ most exciting) event every day.

> **Remember!**
> **Comparative adjectives** compare two things.
>   Francisco's hat is **crazier than** Yin's hat.
>   Maria's costume is **more interesting than** Tara's costume.
> **Superlative adjectives** compare more than two things.
>   Francisco's hat is **the craziest** in the school.
>   Maria's costume is **the most interesting** in her class.

3. The (wild/wilder/wildest) hat in the class wins a prize.

4. The (good/better/best) costume wins a prize.

5. The (busy/busier/busiest) day is going to be "Fun Friday."

6. It is going to be very (crowded / more crowded / most crowded).

1. This year's celebration is going to be bigger than last year's celebration.

2. _____

GRAMMAR

> Learn more in the Grammar Reference, pages 131-141.

A Write sentences in the future tense. Use information from the letter on page 92.

Future Tense with *be going to*	
Affirmative	**Negative**
The school **is going to have** an event every day next week.	The school **isn't going to have** an event on Saturday.
On Friday, students **are going to have** a picnic.	They **aren't going to have** class.

For actions in the future, use *be + going to* + verb.

1. the Oak Street School / have / Fun Time Festival / next week

   The Oak Street School is going to have a Fun Time Festival next week.

2. on Monday / students / meet / at the school / at 7:45 a.m.

   _____

3. on Tuesday / students / have a dance party / at 4:30 in the afternoon

   _____

4. on Wednesday / students / wear crazy hats

   _____

5. on Thursday / some students / wear costumes

   _____

6. Friday / be / the busiest day

   _____

7. on Friday morning / students / not have class

   _____

B Add *would* or *please* to make the sentences more formal.

Requests and Invitations	
Informal	Formal
Francisco **wants to** go to the party. We **want** students **to** wear costumes.	Francisco **would like to** go to the party. We **would like** students **to** wear costumes.
Go to the party with him. **Do** you **want to** come to the party?	**Please** go to the party with him. **Would** you **like to** come to the party?

1. The school wants students to enjoy the Fun Time Festival events.

   <u>The school would like students to enjoy the Fun Time Festival events.</u>

2. We want students to be on time on Monday.

   _____

3. Wear a hat for the contest on Wednesday.

   _____

4. The school wants parents to come early on Friday.

   _____

5. Come to the picnic with us on Friday.

   _____

6. Do you want to come to Friday's events?

   _____

C Compare last year's Fun Time Festival to this year's Fun Time Festival. Use information from the letter on page 92.

1. Last year, students visited a history museum.

   <u>This year, students are going to visit an art museum.</u>

2. Last year, the school had a hip hop dance party.

   _____

3. Last year, there was a prize for the craziest hair on Wednesday.

   _____

4. Last year, the school had the talent show on Friday morning.

   _____

5. Last year's festival was big.

   _____

ORGANIZATION

Chronological Order

Copy the timeline or make one on a computer. Complete the timeline with events from the letter on page 92.

with events from the letter on page 92.

Remember!
Chronological order tells events in time order. Writers often use a timeline to organize events by time.

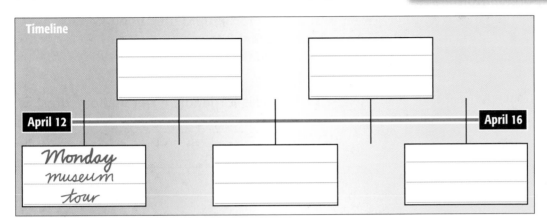

Timeline

April 12 | April 16

Monday museum tour

WRITING STRATEGIES

Form, Audience, Topic, Purpose

Remember!
Use different words and phrases for different types of writing. Before you write, ask questions:
What topic am I writing about? (Is it a fun event? a big problem? an interesting person?)
Who is my audience? (Is the reader a friend? a teacher? someone I don't know?)
What is the purpose? (Am I writing to describe? to explain? to persuade?)
What form should I use? (Should I write a formal letter? a paragraph? an essay?)

Look at the words and phrases. Think about audience and form. Make a two-column chart in your notebook or use a computer. Write each word or phrase in the correct column.

I would like to invite you to a party.		Come to a party.
Hi Marco,	Dear Mr. Griggs:	Sincerely,
Say hi to everyone!	Please give my regards to your family.	Love,
Mary	Mrs. Jones	

Informal Letter	Formal Letter
Come to the party.	

Writing a Formal Letter

Formal letters and friendly letters have different styles (see page 86). Formal letters usually give more background information. In formal letters, writers use more formal language. They do not use contractions. People usually use a formal style for people they don't know. Business letters and event invitations are examples of formal letters.

A Read. Read Jenny's final drafts of her letters. One draft is a friendly letter and one draft is a formal invitation.

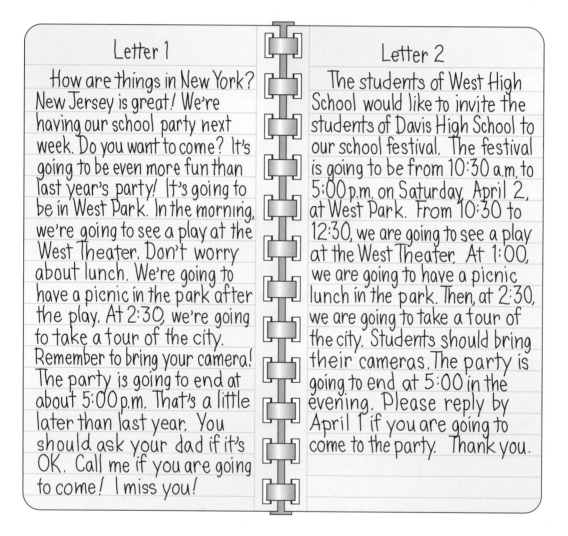

Letter 1

How are things in New York? New Jersey is great! We're having our school party next week. Do you want to come? It's going to be even more fun than last year's party! It's going to be in West Park. In the morning, we're going to see a play at the West Theater. Don't worry about lunch. We're going to have a picnic in the park after the play. At 2:30, we're going to take a tour of the city. Remember to bring your camera! The party is going to end at about 5:00 p.m. That's a little later than last year. You should ask your dad if it's OK. Call me if you are going to come! I miss you!

Letter 2

The students of West High School would like to invite the students of Davis High School to our school festival. The festival is going to be from 10:30 a.m. to 5:00 p.m. on Saturday, April 2, at West Park. From 10:30 to 12:30, we are going to see a play at the West Theater. At 1:00, we are going to have a picnic lunch in the park. Then, at 2:30, we are going to take a tour of the city. Students should bring their cameras. The party is going to end at 5:00 in the evening. Please reply by April 1 if you are going to come to the party. Thank you.

Learn new words. Write them in your personal dictionary.

B Write the body of each letter. Look at the letter forms on page 99. Look at the writing styles in Exercise A. Write a complete draft for each letter. Use the correct form.

A Friendly Letter and a Formal Letter

West High School
1655 Lincoln Dr.
Westwood, NJ 07675

March 29, 2008

Mr. David Parker
Principal
Davis High School
6345 Broadway
Westwood, NJ 07675

Dear Mr. Parker:

Sincerely,

Jenny Lee

Jenny Lee, Class President

March 29, 2008

Hi Maria!

Your friend,
Jenny

STEP-BY-STEP WRITING

Purpose: Invite People to an Event

WRITING PROMPT

Plan an event for your class. Schedule three or more activities for the event. Then, write a formal invitation to another class or school to come to the event. Remember to include the date, location, and start time of the event. Include a short description of activities and the times they start. Finally, ask the contact person to reply to your message.

✔ Prompt Checklist

- ❏ I read the prompt carefully.
- ❏ I understood the form, audience, topic, and purpose of the prompt.

STEP 1 Pre-write

Look at Jenny's timeline. Make a timeline for your event. What would you like to do? When and where would you like to do it?

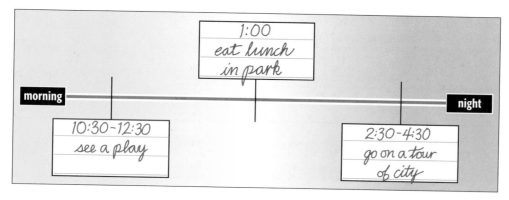

1:00
eat lunch
in park

morning

night

10:30–12:30
see a play

2:30–4:30
go on a tour
of city

STEP 2 Organize

Look at Jenny's letter organizer. Organize your ideas into the correct letter format. Copy the organizer or make one on a computer. Research any information you need.

	Jenny's Letter Organizer
Heading	School address?
	Date?
	Contact person and address?
Greeting	Dear ?
Body	**Date:** April 2
	Location: West Park
	Event start time: 10:30
	Activities and times: 10:30-12:30 see a play at West Theater,
	1:00 eat lunch in West Park, 2:30 go on a city tour
Closing	Sincerely? Your friend?

STEP 3 Draft and Revise

A Practice. **Look at Jenny's first draft. How can she improve it? Answer the questions.**

JENNY'S FIRST DRAFT

Mr. David Parker
6345 Broadway
Westwood, NJ 07675
March 29, 2008

Dear David:

    1) The students of West High School would like to invite the students of Davis High School to our school festival. 2) The festival is going be from 10:30 a.m. to 5:00 p.m. on Saturday, April 2 at West Park. 3) At 1:00, we are going to eat lunch in West Park. 4) From 10:30 to 12:30, we are going to see a play at the West Theater. 5) Then, at 2:30, we are going to take a tour of the city. 6) Students should bring their cameras. 7) The party is going to end at 5:00 in the evening. 8) Let us know by April 1 if you're going to come!

                        Sincerely,

                        Jenny Lee, Class President

---

1. What part of the letter is missing?
   A the heading and the body
   B the date and the greeting
   C the closing and the signature
   D her school's address

2. What should Jenny change the greeting to?
   A Dear Mr. David:
   B Dear Mr. Principal:
   C Dear Mr. Parker:
   D Dear Mr.,

3. What sentence is not in correct chronological order?
   A Sentence 2
   B Sentence 4
   C Sentence 5
   D Sentence 7

4. What is a more formal way to write sentence 8?
   A Reply soon!
   B Please reply by April 1 if you are going to come.
   C We want you to respond by April 1.
   D Would you like to come?

B Draft. **Write a first draft of your invitation. Use your notes from Steps 1 and 2.**

C Revise. **Read your first draft. How can you improve it? Look at the revision checklist. Revise your writing.**

Revision Checklist

- ❏ I used the correct letter form and writing style for the audience, topic, and purpose.
- ❏ I included the date, time, location, and activity information.
- ❏ I listed the activities in chronological order.
- ❏ I asked the contact person to reply.

STEP 4 Edit

A **Practice. Look at the sentences. Choose the best word or phrase to complete each sentence.**

1. Our school has a talent show _____ year.
   A next
   B by
   C last
   Ⓓ every

2. We're going to go to New York City _____ .
   A last weekend
   B on day
   C next weekend
   D by weekend

3. Our event is going to be _____ than their event.
   A craziest
   B interesting

   C biggest
   D more interesting

4. John _____ on Saturday.
   A is going to stay home
   B going to stay home
   C staying home
   D is staying

5. _____ to the party, Mrs. Rios?
   A Come
   B Do you want to come
   C Would like to come
   D Would you like to come

B **Edit. Reread your draft from Step 3. Look at the editing checklist. Edit your writing.**

C **Peer Edit. Exchange drafts with a partner. Tell your partner what you like about the draft. Look at the editing checklist. Tell your partner how to improve the draft.**

Editing Checklist

	my	
me	partner	
☐	☐	used event words, time expressions, and adjectives correctly
☐	☐	used future tense, formal requests and invitations correctly
☐	☐	used correct spelling, punctuation, and capitalization

STEP 5 Publish

Write your invitation letter in your best handwriting or on a computer. Look at Jenny's letters on pages 98 and 99 for ideas. Remember to include all the parts of a letter and the event details. Present your letter to the class.

TECHNOLOGY

Finding Local Events

Do a keyword search for the name of your town and state with the exact phrase "event schedule." You may need to narrow your search. Click on hyperlinks to find five future events you would like to attend. Write a list of the events and the information for each. Cite your sources. Then, write an invitation to a teacher to join you and your family at an event. Use the correct form.

GROUP WRITING

Work in a group to write a letter about one of these topics.

1. Choose a topic.
2. Decide the letter form.
3. Do research if you need to.
4. Write a first draft.
5. Revise and edit the letter with your group.
6. Present your group's letter to the class.

Topic 1

Invite a friend or family member to the event below. Write about three activities you would like to attend.

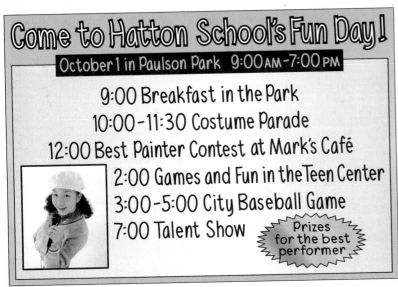

Come to Hatton School's Fun Day!

October 1 in Paulson Park   9:00 AM – 7:00 PM

9:00 Breakfast in the Park
10:00 – 11:30 Costume Parade
12:00 Best Painter Contest at Mark's Café
2:00 Games and Fun in the Teen Center
3:00 – 5:00 City Baseball Game
7:00 Talent Show   *Prizes for the best performer*

Topic 2

Write a letter to the teacher below. Request more information. Ask *wh-* questions to find out the time and location of the lessons.

FREE STUDENT STUDY SESSIONS

The Mayfield High School
English Department
is going to offer free
English lessons this summer.

*Please write
for more information.*

Mrs. Wells, Head English Teacher
Mayfield High School
3246 West 5th Street
Newbury, AZ 02200

TIMED WRITING

Choose one writing prompt. Complete the writing task in 45 minutes.

WRITING PROMPT 1

Write a letter or e-mail to a friend. Describe three interesting things you did last week. Use chronological order to describe the activities. Think about form, audience, topic, and purpose.

WRITING PROMPT 2

Plan an event for your class. Write a letter to the principal of your school. Tell your name, your age, and what grade you are in. Persuade your principal to come to the event. Tell the time and location of the event. Write about the activities. Think about form, audience, topic, and purpose.

Test Tip

Find your purpose! Look for words like **explain**, **describe**, and **persuade**. They tell you the purpose of a writing prompt.

SELF-CHECK

Think about your writing skills. Check (✔) the answers that are true.

1. I understand...
   - ❏ the days of the week.
   - ❏ free time activities.
   - ❏ time expressions.
   - ❏ feelings and moods.
   - ❏ event words.
   - ❏ comparative adjectives.

2. I can correctly use...
   - ❏ simple past tense with regular verbs.
   - ❏ simple past tense with *be* and *have*.
   - ❏ future tense with *going to*.
   - ❏ polite requests and invitations.

3. I can correctly...
   - ❏ write mailing addresses.
   - ❏ identify the form, audience, topic, and purpose of my writing.

4. I can organize...
   - ❏ by the parts of a letter.
   - ❏ by chronological order.

5. I can write...
   - ❏ informal letters.
   - ❏ formal letters.

Unit 9

Tell a Story

UNIT OBJECTIVES

Writing
personal narrative

Organization
beginning, middle, and end of
a story

Writing Strategies
time transition words

Vocabulary
travel and transportation words
synonyms and antonyms for
adjectives

Grammar
simple past tense of irregular
verbs
wh- questions with the past tense

Technology
finding specific information

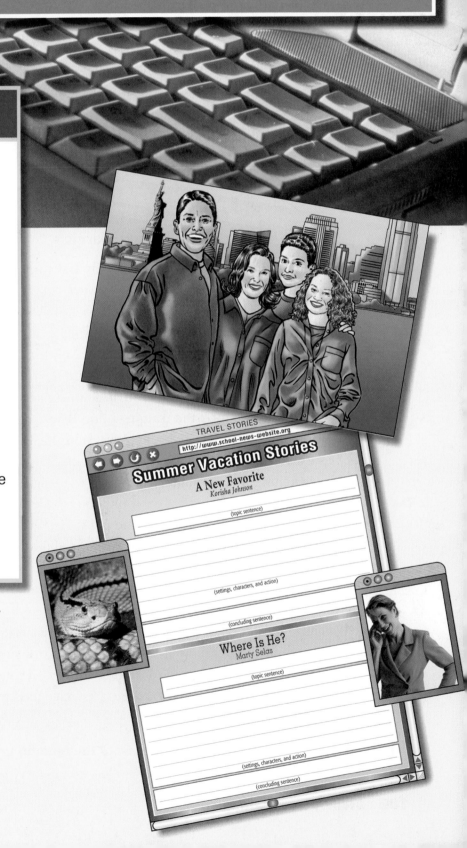

TRAVEL STORIES

http://www.school-news-website.org

Summer Vacation Stories

A New Favorite
Korisha Johnson

(topic sentence)

(settings, characters, and action)

(concluding sentence)

Where Is He?
Marty Selas

(topic sentence)

(settings, characters, and action)

(concluding sentence)

READING

A **Discuss.** **Plan a trip with a partner. Answer the questions. Present your travel plans to the class.**

1. Where are you going to go? _____
2. When are you going to go there? _____
3. Who are you going to go with? _____
4. How are you going to get there?
   ❑ train   ❑ bus   ❑ car   ❑ other _____
5. What are you going to do?
   ❑ go sightseeing   ❑ go to a museum   ❑ buy souvenirs
   ❑ visit friends or family   ❑ other _____
6. Why do you want to go there? _____

B **Read.** **Read about the Garcia family's trip to New York City.**

Our New York Adventure
Francisco Garcia

Learn new words. Write them in your personal dictionary.

My family took a trip to New York City last summer. We visited my mother's friends, Mr. and Mrs. Vega. We were very excited before we left. It was our first trip to New York. We flew to New York on Sunday morning. The weather was clear and sunny. The airplane was very comfortable. We arrived at about 3:00 p.m. Mr. and Mrs. Vega met us at the airport. We stayed with Mr. and Mrs. Vega for one week.

We didn't have much free time during our visit to New York. We were busy. On Monday, we took the train to Long Beach. We swam and ate watermelon. The next day, we took a ferry and saw the Statue of Liberty. The view was amazing. We had an exciting time. However, one day was especially exciting for Maria. On Friday, we went sightseeing. First, we took a subway into the city. Later on, we took a bus to Central Park. The bus was very crowded. We got off the bus at the park. However, something was strange. Maria wasn't with us. We looked around and finally we saw her. Maria was on the bus! She didn't get off. There were too many people. My father ran after the bus. At last, the driver stopped and Maria got off. In the end, Maria was safe. She was very careful on buses and trains after that.

We came back to Los Angeles the next day. Mr. and Mrs. Vega drove us to the airport in their car. We got home late Saturday evening. We were exhausted, but we were happy. We had a wonderful time in New York. However, Maria is never going to forget her scary bus trip.

C **Write captions.** **Write a sentence from the reading under each picture on page 107. Use sentences from the passage.**

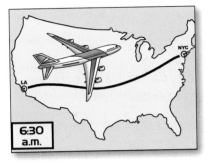

1. My family took a trip to New York City last summer.

2. _____

3. _____

4. _____

5. _____

6. _____

7. _____

8. _____

9. _____

10. _____

VOCABULARY

A Unscramble the letters to make types of transportation. Find the words in the reading on page 106. Write the complete sentences.

1. arilapne _____airplane_____ The airplane was very comfortable._____

2. ratin _____ _____

3. refry _____ _____

4. yabuws _____ _____

5. usb _____ _____

6. rac _____ _____

B Find the words from the box in the reading on page 106. Complete the chart with the synonyms and antonyms. Then write the complete sentences.

Remember!
Synonyms are words that have the same (or close to the same) meanings. Antonyms are words that have opposite meanings. Good writers use different words to make their writing interesting.

synonyms	very good	=	great
antonyms	big	≠	small

careful	~~exciting~~	exhausted	wonderful	clear	scary
~~amazing~~	safe	strange	comfortable	crowded	sunny

Synonyms		Antonyms	
very interesting	1. amazing	boring	7. exciting
unusual	2.	cloudy	8.
frightening	3.	empty	9.
very good	4.	careless	10.
very tired	5.	in danger	11.
bright	6.	uncomfortable	12.

1. The view was amazing.

2.

C Reread the passage on page 106. Then match these words to make travel phrases.

1. take ___e___	a. back to Los Angeles
2. visit _____	b. a car to the airport
3. fly _____	c. to New York
4. arrive _____	d. at 3:00 p.m.
5. meet _____	e. ~~a trip~~
6. go _____	f. sightseeing
7. get _____	g. off a bus
8. come _____	h. someone at the airport
9. drive _____	i. friends in another city

GRAMMAR

➤ Learn more in the Grammar Reference, pages 131–141.

A Write the past tense form for each irregular verb. Then find each verb in the reading on page 106. Write the complete sentence.

Simple Past Tense of Irregular Verbs		
Verb	**Affirmative**	**Negative**
take	They took a trip to New York.	They didn't take a trip to San Francisco.
fly	We flew to New York.	They didn't fly to Portland.
meet	They met us at the airport.	They didn't meet us at the bus station.

1. take ___took___	8. see _____
2. are _____	9. have _____
3. is _____	10. go _____
4. fly _____	11. run _____
5. meet _____	12. come _____
6. swim _____	13. drive _____
7. eat _____	14. get _____

1. My family took a trip to New York City last summer.

2.

B Complete the questions with the correct forms of the verbs in parentheses. Answer the questions. Use information from the reading on page 106.

Wh- Questions with Past Tense	
Present Tense	**Past Tense**
Where does the Garcia family **take** their summer trip every year? **Why do** they **go** there? **How do** they **get** there? **Who do** they **visit** there? **What do** they **see** there? **When do** they **come** home?	**Where did** the Garcia family **take** their summer trip last year? **Why did** they **go** there? **How did** they **get** there? **Who did** they **visit** there? **What did** they **see** there? **When did** they **come** home?

1. (go) Where __did__ the Garcia family __go__? ____They went to New York City.____

2. (get) How _____ they _____ to New York City? _____

3. (eat) What _____ they _____ at Long Beach? _____

4. (get) Where _____ Francisco _____ off the bus? _____

5. (run) Why _____ Mr. Garcia _____ after the bus? _____

6. (go) Who _____ the Garcia family _____ to the airport with? _____

7. (come) When _____ they _____ home? _____

C Complete the paragraph. Use the past tense of the verbs in parentheses. There are regular and irregular verbs.

The Garcia family (1. take) __took__ a trip to New York City. They
(2. fly) _____ to New York on Sunday. They (3. arrive) _____ at 3:00 in
the afternoon. Mr. and Mrs. Vega (4. meet) _____ them at the airport.
They (5. not have) _____ a lot of free time in New York. They (6. swim)
_____ at Long Beach. They also (7. see) _____ the Statue of Liberty.
On Friday, the Garcia family (8. go) _____ to Central Park on a bus. The
Garcia family (9. get) _____ off the bus. However, Maria (10. not get)
_____ off. In the end, Maria (11. is) _____ safe. The Garcia family
(12. come) _____ home on Sunday. Mr. and Mrs. Vega (13. drive)
_____ them to the airport. They (14. are) _____ exhausted, but happy
after their trip. They (15. have) _____ a wonderful time in New York.

ORGANIZATION

Beginning, Middle, and End of a Story

Find the beginning, the middle, and the end of the passage on page 106. Write two sentences from each part of the story in the chart below.

Remember!
Stories have a beginning, a middle, and an end. The beginning introduces the story and tells about the setting and characters. The middle gives details about the action or plot of the story. The end tells what the story means or why it is important.

Story Organizer
Beginning
1. My family took a trip to New York City last summer.
2.
Middle
3.
4.
End
5.
6.

WRITING STRATEGIES

Time Transition Words

Add the correct time transition word or phrase to each sentence. Use information from the reading on page 106.

Remember!
Transition words help to connect ideas. Time transition words tell the reader the order of events in a story. Look at how time transition words can change the meaning of a sentence.
Zhi studied **after** he ate lunch.
Zhi studied **before** he ate lunch.

during	later on	in the end	the next day
at last	~~before~~	after that	finally

1. The Garcia family was very excited _____before_____ the trip.

2. They didn't have a lot of free time _____ their visit to New York.

3. On Monday, they took a train. _____, they took a ferry.

4. On Friday, they took a subway to the city. _____, they took a bus to Central Park.

5. After they got off the bus, they looked for Maria. _____, they saw her.

6. Mr. Garcia ran after the bus. _____ the driver stopped.

7. _____, Maria was safe.

8. Maria was very careful on buses and trains _____.

Personal Narrative

A personal narrative **tells a story from the author's** point of view. **It uses the** first person
(*I, my, me, we, our, us*). **It also has a beginning, a middle, and an end. In a narrative
paragraph, the** topic sentence **introduces the story. The** supporting sentences **tell about
the setting, characters, and action. The** concluding sentence **ends the story and tells what it
means. Travel stories and journal entries are examples of personal narratives.**

 A **Read. Read the stories about trips.**

Learn new
words. Write
them in your
personal
dictionary.

My family took a trip to San Francisco last July. My mother, my sister Bethany,
and I visited my aunt and uncle. We took a train from Portland, Oregon to Oakland,
California. Oakland is a city near San Francisco. We left on Wednesday morning.
We were on the train all day. It was amazing. We saw a lot of beautiful mountains
and trees during the trip. However, we arrived very late that night. We were
exhausted. We got off the train, but something was strange. My uncle was not at
the station. My mother was really worried. Finally, my mother's cell phone rang.
It was my uncle. He was at the Emeryville station. We were at the Oakland station.
He was at the wrong station. He drove quickly to the Oakland Station. We were
really happy to see him. In the end, our trip was fantastic. We're going to go again
next year. I hope my uncle goes to the correct station next time.

I had an interesting trip last July. My mother, father, brother, and I went to a
new zoo downtown. My father drove us to the zoo. It was very close to our home.
We walked around the zoo after we arrived. We saw many animals. Some animals
were beautiful. Some animals were funny. I really liked the snakes. I thought they
were fascinating. My brother didn't like them. He thought they were scary. Later
on, we watched an animal show. During the show, the zookeeper gave me a snake!
I held it for five minutes. It was really heavy, but it was beautiful. Later on, my
brother held the snake, too. Now, he doesn't think they are scary. They are his new
favorite animal. In the end, we all had a good time at the zoo.

 B **Find the author. Reread the paragraphs.** (Circle) the topic sentence in each paragraph.
Underline the supporting sentences. Make a box around the concluding sentence. Then,
write each paragraph under the correct name and title on page 113.

Personal Narratives

TRAVEL STORIES

http://www.school-news-website.org

Summer Vacation Stories

A New Favorite
Korisha Johnson

(topic sentence)

(settings, characters, and action)

(concluding sentence)

Where Is He?
Marty Selas

(topic sentence)

(settings, characters, and action)

(concluding sentence)

Purpose: Tell a Story

WRITING PROMPT

Tell a story about a trip you took. Write a personal narrative paragraph for a class Web site. Describe the setting and the characters. Describe the action. Use transition words to connect ideas. Be sure your story has a beginning, a middle, and an end.

✔ Prompt Checklist

❏ I read the task carefully.
❏ I understand the form, audience, topic, and purpose of the prompt.

STEP 1 Pre-write

Look at Marty's story planner. Copy the chart or make one on a computer. Think about the information you need. Write notes for your paragraph.

Marty's Story Planner
Title
My Trip?
Setting
Where did you go? San Francisco   **When did you go?** last summer
Characters
Who did you go with? me, my mother, and my sister
Action
What happened? We arrived and my uncle was not at the train station.

STEP 2 Organize

Look at Marty's story organizer. Organize your ideas. Copy the story organizer or make one on a computer. Complete the story organizer with information about your story.

Marty's Story Organizer
Beginning
I went to San Francisco last summer. My mother and sister came, too. We...
Middle
We left on Wednesday. We arrive late at night. My uncle was not...
End
We were happy to see him.

MARTY'S FIRST DRAFT

1) My mother, my sister Bethany, and I visited my aunt and uncle. 2) We took a train from Portland, Oregon to Oakland, California. 3) Oakland is a city near San Francisco. 4) We left on Wednesday morning. 5) We were on the train all day. 6) It was very nice. 7) We saw a lot of beautiful mountains and trees during the trip. 8) However, we arrived very late that night. 9) We were exhausted. 11) We got off the train. 12) Something was strange. 13) My uncle was not at the station. 14) My mother's cell phone rang. 15) My uncle was at the Emeryville station. 16) We were at the Oakland station. 17) He drove quickly to the Oakland Station. 18) He was at the wrong station. 19) We were really happy to see him. 20) Our trip was fantastic. 21) We're going to go again next year. 22) I hope my uncle goes to the correct station.

---

1. Which topic sentence should Marty insert before sentence 1?

   A My trip.

   B I went to San Francisco.

   Ⓒ My family took a trip to San Francisco last July.

   D San Francisco is a city.

2. How can Marty change sentence 6 to make it more interesting?

   A It was terrible.

   B It was amazing.

   C It was OK.

   D It was exhausting.

3. What two sentences are not in the correct chronological order?

   A Sentence 13 and Sentence 14

   B Sentence 14 and Sentence 15

   C Sentence 16 and Sentence 17

   D Sentence 17 and Sentence 18

4. What time transition should Marty insert in sentence 20?

   A Before,

   B Finally,

   C In the end,

   D During,

B Draft. **Write a first draft of your narrative paragraph. Use your notes from Steps 1 and 2.**

C Revise. **Read your first draft. How can you improve it? Look at the revision checklist. Revise your writing.**

☑ Revision Checklist

- ❑ My story has a clear beginning, middle, and end.
- ❑ I described the setting, characters, and action.
- ❑ I used transition words to help the story flow smoothly.

STEP 4 Edit

A Practice. **Look at the sentences. Choose the best substitute for the underlined words. If the sentence is correct, choose "Make no change."**

1. My family took a train to Chicago last summer.
   A took train
   B drove a train
   C flew a train
   D Make no change. ✓

2. The scary movie was bright.
   A cloudy
   B frightening
   C careful
   D Make no change.

3. Later on, we eat lunch at a new cafe.
   A eats
   B did ate
   C ate
   D Make no change.

4. We didn't swam on our trip.
   A doesn't swam
   B didn't swim
   C doesn't swim
   D Make no change.

5. Where do you go last weekend?
   A Where do go
   B Where did you go
   C Where you go
   D Make no change.

B Edit. **Reread your draft from Step 3. Look at the editing checklist. Edit your writing.**

C Peer Edit. **Exchange drafts with a partner. Tell your partner what you like about the draft. Look at the editing checklist. Tell your partner how to improve the draft.**

✓ Editing Checklist

me	my partner	
☐	☐	used travel words and adjectives correctly
☐	☐	used the simple past tense correctly
☐	☐	used correct spelling, punctuation, and capitalization

STEP 5 Publish

Rewrite your paragraph in your notebook or on a computer. Present your paragraph to the class. Who has the most interesting story? Why is it interesting to you?

TECHNOLOGY

Finding Specific Information

Do an **keyword search** for "Statue of Liberty" and "visitor information." How do you get there? When is it open? Write down the hours of Liberty Park and how much the ferry ride costs. Cite your source. Then find visitor information for an interesting place in your city.

Unit 10

Summarize Information

Rosa Parks

Dawn Greene

Rosa Parks was an important (1) civil rights activist in America.

She was born in (2) _____ , Alabama on

(3) _____ , 1913. Rosa moved to

(4) _____ , Alabama in 1924.

Then, in (5) _____ , Rosa married

Raymond Parks. Raymond was interested in the civil rights movement.

Rosa wanted people to have equal rights, too. In 1943, Rosa joined the

(6) _____ . On (7) _____ ,

1955, Rosa refused to give her seat on the bus to a white person.

The police arrested Rosa. This caused many changes in America.

It taught Americans that all people are equal. Rosa Parks died in

(8) 20 _____ , but many people still admire her.

They think she was very brave and strong.

Baine, Reggie. *The History of the Civil Rights Movement.* Boston: Heinle & Heinle, 2006. pp. 26-29.

A **Discuss.** **Answer the questions. Report your information to the class.**

1. What does the word *hero* mean? _____

2. Who is your hero? _____

3. What information do you know about that person? _____

4. Why is that person a hero to you? _____

B **Read.** **Read Francisco's essay about his grandfather.**

> **Learn new words. Write them in your personal dictionary.**

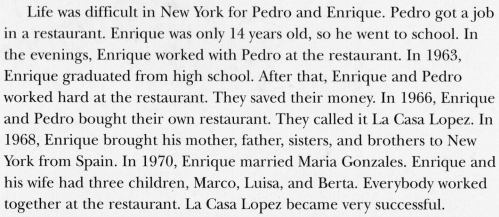

My Hero
by Francisco Garcia

My hero is Enrique Lopez. Enrique Lopez was born on October 1, 1945. Enrique grew up in a small town in Spain. He lived with his mother, father, three sisters, and four brothers. Enrique's family was happy, but they didn't have a lot of money. So, in 1959, Enrique and his brother Pedro moved to New York.

Life was difficult in New York for Pedro and Enrique. Pedro got a job in a restaurant. Enrique was only 14 years old, so he went to school. In the evenings, Enrique worked with Pedro at the restaurant. In 1963, Enrique graduated from high school. After that, Enrique and Pedro worked hard at the restaurant. They saved their money. In 1966, Enrique and Pedro bought their own restaurant. They called it La Casa Lopez. In 1968, Enrique brought his mother, father, sisters, and brothers to New York from Spain. In 1970, Enrique married Maria Gonzales. Enrique and his wife had three children, Marco, Luisa, and Berta. Everybody worked together at the restaurant. La Casa Lopez became very successful.

Enrique and his family still live in New York. Enrique doesn't work at the restaurant now, but he is very busy. He teaches English classes for new immigrants every afternoon. Next year, he is going to open a cooking school, too. He and Pedro are going to teach the classes. Enrique didn't win any big prizes and he isn't famous. However, many people admire him. He always helps people and he is very kind. Enrique's daughter Berta is proud of her father. Berta lives in Los Angeles with her husband, son, and daughter. She often tells her family about Enrique. That is why Enrique Lopez is my hero. Enrique Lopez is my grandfather.

 C **Write captions.** **Write a sentence from the reading under each picture on page 119. Use sentences from the reading.**

1. Enrique Lopez was born on October 1, 1945.

2. _____

3. _____

4. _____

5. _____

6. _____

7. _____

8. _____

9. _____

10. _____

VOCABULARY

A Find these words and phrases in the reading on page 118. Write the complete sentences.

was born	grew up	moved to	got a job	graduated from
married	had children	saved money	became successful	admire

1. Enrique Lopez was born on October 1, 1945.

2. _____

3. _____

4. _____

5. _____

6. _____

7. _____

8. _____

9. _____

10. _____

B Unscramble the letters to find family words.

1. rafghtedarn grandfather

2. ilncehrd _____

3. hubnads _____

4. fiew _____

5. osn _____

6. taergdhu _____

7. issret _____

8. threbor _____

C Write five sentences about Francisco's family. Use words from vocabulary Activity B and sentences from the reading on page 118.

1. <u>Enrique Lopez is Francisco's grandfather.</u>

2. _____

3. _____

4. _____

5. _____

GRAMMAR ► Learn more in the Grammar Reference, pages 131-141.

A Answer the questions. Write complete sentences. Use the correct verb tense.

Simple Verb Tenses	
Present	Enrique **lives** in New York
Past	He **moved** to New York in 1959.
Future	He **is going to open** a cooking school next year.

1. Who is Francisco's hero?

   <u>Enrique Lopez is Francisco's hero.</u>

2. Where is Enrique Lopez from?

   _____

3. When was he born?

   _____

4. What did Enrique do in 1959?

   _____

5. What happened in 1966?

   _____

6. How many children did Enrique have?

   _____

7. What does Enrique do every afternoon?

   _____

8. What is Enrique going to do next year?

   _____

B Check the subject-verb agreement in these sentences. Four sentences are incorrect. Mark the incorrect sentences. Rewrite the incorrect sentences correctly.

Subject-Verb Agreement		
	Present Tense	**Future Tense**
I	I **live** in Los Angeles.	I **am going to give** cooking lessons.
You/We/They	Francisco and his family **live** in Los Angeles.	Enrique and Pedro **are going to give** cooking lessons.
He/She/It	Enrique **lives** in New York.	Enrique **is going to open** a school next year.

1. Enrique Lopez ~~are~~ Francisco's hero. S/V

2. Enrique and his Family live in New York City.

3. Enrique don't work at the restaurant now.

4. He teaches English classes.

5. Next year, Enrique and his brother is going to open a school.

6. They are going to give cooking lessons.

7. Enrique's daughter Berta and her family lives in Los Angeles.

8. Berta is very proud of her father.

1. Enrique Lopez is Francisco's hero.

C Complete the summary. Use the correct forms of the verbs in parentheses.

Enrique Lopez (1) <u>was born</u> (is born) on October 1, 1945. In 1959, he (2) _____ (move) to the United States from Spain with his brother. He (2) _____ (go) to school and his brother (3) _____ (work) in a restaurant. In 1963, Enrique (4) _____ (graduate) from high school. He and his brother (5) _____ (buy) a restaurant in 1966. His family (6) _____ (come) to New York City in 1968. He (7) _____ (marry) Maria Gonzales in 1970. Now, the Lopez family (8) _____ (live) in New York City. Enrique (9) _____ (not work) at the restaurant. He (10) _____ (teach) English classes. Next year, he (11) _____ (open) a school. He and his brother (11) _____ (teach) cooking lessons. Many people (12) _____ (admire) Enrique because he (13) _____ (is) helpful and kind.

ORGANIZATION

Summary Paragraph

Reread the passage on page 118. Take notes. Then paraphrase the main ideas in each paragraph. Use your own words.

Topic Sentence: Enrique Lopez is Francisco's hero.		
Passage	Main ideas	Paraphrased information
Paragraph 1	born in 1945 – Spain 1959 - to New York with brother	Enrique Lopez was born in 1945 in Spain. In 1959, he moved to America with his brother.
Paragraph 2		
Paragraph 3		

WRITING CONVENTIONS

Citing Sources

Label the source citation with words from the box.

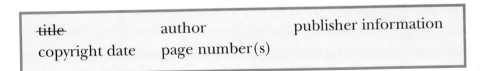

title   author   publisher information
copyright date   page number(s)

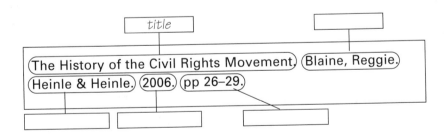

Writing a summary

A summary gives the facts and main ideas from a longer passage or story. Writers often summarize research information from encyclopedias, reference books, and other resources. They only include information that is important to the topic.

  Read. Read the encyclopedia entry about Rosa Parks.

> ## A Biography of Rosa Parks
>
> Rosa Louise McCauley was born on February 4, 1913 in Tuskegee, Alabama. In 1924, at age 11, Rosa moved to Montgomery, Alabama to study. She went to The Industrial School for Girls. Five years later, Rosa quit school to help her grandmother. In 1932, Rosa married Raymond Parks. Rosa's husband encouraged Rosa to finish school. She graduated from high school in 1933.
>
> Rosa's husband, Raymond, was an active member of the National Association for the Advancement of Colored People (NAACP). NAACP members supported civil rights. They wanted black people and white people to be treated equally. However, at the time, black people and white people were often segregated. They did not eat in the same restaurants. They did not ride the bus together. On buses, white people sat in the front of the bus. Black people stood, or sat in the back of the bus. Rosa Parks thought this was wrong, so in 1943, she joined the NAACP.
>
> On December 1, 1955 Rosa Parks changed America. She boarded a bus and sat down. Soon, a white man got on the bus. The bus driver asked Rosa to move. Rosa Parks was tired from working all day. She said, "no." The police came and arrested Rosa. The black people of Alabama were very angry. They stopped riding buses and the bus companies lost a lot of money. Finally, the segregation laws were changed. Black people could sit where they wanted to.
>
> Rosa Parks died in 2005, but many people still admire her. She is often thought to be one of America's strongest and bravest civil rights activists. Rosa's actions helped Americans to understand that black people and white people should have equal civil rights. Because of this, Rosa Parks is sometimes called "the mother of the civil rights movement."

Learn new words. Write them in your personal dictionary.

 Find information. Find information in the encyclopedia entry to complete the summary on page 125. Rewrite the summary with the correct information.

A Summary

Rosa Parks

Dawn Greene

Rosa Parks was an important (1) <u>civil rights activist</u> in America.

She was born in (2) _____ , Alabama on

(3) _____ , 1913. Rosa moved to

(4) _____ , Alabama in 1924.

Then, in (5) _____ , Rosa married

Raymond Parks. Raymond was interested in the civil rights movement.

Rosa wanted people to have equal rights, too. In 1943, Rosa joined the

(6) _____ . On (7) _____ ,

1955, Rosa refused to give her seat on the bus to a white person.

The police arrested Rosa. This caused many changes in America.

It taught Americans that all people are equal. Rosa Parks died in

(8) 20 _____ , but many people still admire her.

They think she was very brave and strong.

Baine, Reggie. *The History of the Civil Rights Movement.* Boston: Heinle & Heinle, 2006. pp. 26-29.

Rosa Parks was an important civil rights activist in

America. She was . . .

STEP–BY–STEP WRITING

Purpose: Summarize Information

WRITING PROMPT

Look up a famous hero in an encyclopedia or reference book. Write a one-paragraph summary of the information you find. Tell where and when the person was born. Give dates for two or more important events in the person's life. Include the main details about one important thing the person did.

✔ **Prompt Checklist**

- ☐ I read the prompt carefully.
- ☐ I understand the form, audience, topic, and purpose of the prompt.

STEP 1 Pre-write

Read your reference passage. Then, look at Dawn's reading chart. Make your own chart. Read your information again. Find the main ideas from each paragraph.

Dawn's Reading Chart	
Topic: Rosa Parks	
Source	Main ideas
Paragraph 1	February 4, 1913 - born in Alabama
	1924 - moved to Montgomery
	1932 - married …
Paragraph 2	
Paragraph 3	
Paragraph 4	

STEP 2 Organize

Look at Dawn's sentence organizer. Copy the organizer or make one on your computer. Paraphrase your notes. Complete the organizer with sentences for your biography.

Dawn's Sentence Organizer	
Topic Sentence: Rosa Parks was an important person.	
Reading Notes	Paraphrased Sentences
February 4, 1913 - born in Alabama	She was born in Alabama on February 4, 1913.
1924- Montgomery	She moved to Montgomery, Alabama in 1924.
1932 - married …	She married…

STEP 3 Draft and Revise

DAWN'S FIRST DRAFT

(1) Rosa Parks was an important person. (2) She was born in Tuskegee, Alabama on February 4, 1913. (3) She moved to Montgomery, Alabama in 1924. (4) She went to the Industrial School for Girls. (5) In 1932, Rosa married Raymond Parks. (6) Raymond was interested in the civil right movement. (7) In 1943, Rosa joined the National Association for the Advancement of Colored People. (8) On December 1, 1955, Rosa refused to give up her seat. (9) The police arrested Rosa. (10) This caused many changes in America. (11) It taught Americans that all people are equal. (12) Rosa Parks died in 2005, but many people still admire her. (13) They think she was very brave and strong.

A Practice. **Look at Dawn's first draft. How can she improve it? Answer the questions.**

1. What is a better topic sentence?
   A Rosa Louise McCauley was an important person.
   Ⓑ Rosa Parks was a famous civil rights activist.
   C The NAACP was important.
   D Rosa Parks was from Montgomery, Alabama.

2. What sentence is not important or related to the topic sentence?
   A Sentence 1   B Sentence 2
   C Sentence 3   D Sentence 4

3. Where is the best place to add this information?
   | Rosa wanted all people to have equal rights. |
   A after Sentence 4   B after Sentence 5
   C after Sentence 6   D after Sentence 7

4. What is a clearer way to write the underlined part of sentence 8?
   A give her seat on the bus.   B give her seat to a person.
   C give her seat on the bus to a white person. D give the bus to a white person.

B Draft. **Write a first draft of your summary paragraph. Use your notes from Steps 1 and 2.**

C Revise. **Read your first draft. How can you improve it? Look at the revision checklist. Revise your writing.**

✓ Revision Checklist

❑ I told when and where the person was born.
❑ I gave dates about important events in the person's life.
❑ I included details about one important thing the person did.

STEP 4 Edit

A **Practice. Look at the sentences. Choose the best word or phrase to complete each sentence.**

1. My sister _____ Mexico.

   A born in
   Ⓑ was born in
   C is-born in
   D was born on

2. My mother's father is my _____.

   A grandmother
   B cousin
   C father
   D grandfather

3. Rena _____ to school in San Francisco last year.

   A go
   B goes
   C went
   D is going to go

4. Sheri _____ in Dallas, Texas.

   A live
   B lives
   C are
   D don't live

5. Peter and Mark _____ visit me next year.

   A is going to
   B are going
   C is going
   D are going to

B **Edit. Reread your draft from Step 3. Look at the editing checklist. Edit your writing.**

C **Peer Edit. Exchange drafts with a partner. Tell your partner what you like about the draft. Look at the editing checklist. Tell your partner how to improve the draft.**

STEP 5 Publish

Write your summary in your best handwriting or on a computer. Look at Dawn's paragraph on page 125 for ideas. Remember to include a title, your name, and your source information. Present your summary to the class.

☑ Editing Checklist

me	my partner	
☐	☐	used life event and family words correctly
☐	☐	used correct verb tenses and subject-verb agreement
☐	☐	used correct spelling, punctuation, and capitalization

TECHNOLOGY

Finding Reliable Sources

Not all Internet information is reliable. You cannot believe everything you read. The most reliable sources for information are organizations and universities. These Web site addresses end with ".org" or ".edu". Do a keyword search for Rosa Parks. Find one .org site and one .edu site about her. Find three pieces of information about Rosa Parks from each. Cite your Internet sources.

GROUP WRITING

Work in a group to write about one of these topics.

1. Choose a topic.
2. Study the information.
3. Research needed information.
4. Write a first draft.
5. Revise and edit the draft with your group.
6. Present your group's writing to the class.

Topic 1

Write a story about the picture. Tell about the characters, setting, and action. Be sure your story has a beginning, a middle and an end.

Topic 2

Research one of the people below. Write a one-paragraph summary of their life.

Abraham Lincoln

Martin Luther King, Jr.

Anne Frank

TIMED WRITING

Choose one writing prompt. Complete the writing task in 45 minutes.

WRITING PROMPT 1

Think about an event that changed your life. Write a personal narrative paragraph about what happened. Use descriptive adjectives to describe the setting and the characters. Describe the action. Use transition words to connect ideas. Be sure your story has a beginning, a middle, and an end.

WRITING PROMPT 2

Think about someone you know that you think is a hero. Write a one-paragraph summary about the person for a school newspaper. Give dates for two or more important events in the person's life. Tell why you think the person is a hero. Include details to support your information.

> **Test Tip**
>
> **Don't panic!** Sometimes even good writers can't think during a test. Put down your pencil. Relax. Then start again.

SELF-CHECK

Think about your writing skills. Check (✔) the answers that are true.

1. I understand…
   - ❑ travel and transportation words.
   - ❑ synonyms and antonyms for adjectives.
   - ❑ life event words.
   - ❑ extended family words.

2. I can correctly use…
   - ❑ simple past tense of irregular verbs.
   - ❑ *Wh-* questions in the past tense.
   - ❑ all forms of simple tense.
   - ❑ the right verb for the subject.

3. I can correctly…
   - ❑ use time transitions.
   - ❑ cite sources.

4. I can organize my writing by…
   - ❑ telling the beginning, the middle and the end of a story.
   - ❑ writing a summary.

5. I can write to…
   - ❑ tell a personal story.
   - ❑ summarize.

NOUNS

Nouns name a person, place, or thing.

Regular Plural Nouns (p. 16)

Nouns can be singular (*one*) or plural (*more than one*).

To make most nouns plural, add an *s* or *es* after the singular noun.

Singular	Plural	Rule
bedroom book	bedrooms books	most nouns: add **s**
class lunch	classes lunches	nouns that end in **s, ch, sh, x,** or **z**: add **es**
family lady	families ladies	nouns that end in a **consonant + y**: change the **y** to **i** and add **es**

Irregular Plural Nouns

Some nouns are **irregular** in the plural form.

Singular	Irregular Plural
man	men
woman	women
child	children
mouse	mice
foot	feet
tooth	teeth

Count and Noncount Nouns (p. 32)

Count nouns are nouns you can count. They are singular or plural.

Use a, an, the, or a number with count nouns.

Noncount nouns can't be counted. They are singular.

Don't use a, an, or numbers. Use some for a non-specific amount.

Count	Noncount
I have a banana.	I have lettuce.
I have eight oranges.	Buy some cheese.
Cut up the tomato.	Cut up some cheese.

Articles (p. 4)

Use an article before count nouns.

Article	Rule	Example
a, an	before general, singular count nouns use *a* before consonants use *an* before vowels	Francisco is **a** student. There is **a** book. I eat **an** apple every day.
the	before specific nouns when there is only one	I saw a movie. **The** movie was good. There is **the** Lincoln Memorial.

Possessive Nouns (p. 18)

Possessive nouns show ownership.

Sentence	Sentence with Possessive Noun	Rule
Francisco has a small bedroom.	**Francisco's** bedroom is small.	Add apostrophe + s ('s) to names.
The **boy** has a new poster.	The **boy's** poster is new.	Add apostrophe + s ('s) to singular nouns.
The **girls** have gym class now.	The **girls'** gym class is now.	Add apostrophe (') to regular plural nouns.
The **men** have blue hats.	The **men's** hats are blue.	Add apostrophe + s ('s) to irregular plural nouns.

PRONOUNS

A **pronoun** takes the place of a noun or refers to a noun.

Example: <u>My brother</u> is sick today. <u>He</u> has a cold.

Subject Pronouns (p. 6)

Subject pronouns take the place of subject nouns. They do the action in a sentence.

Subject Pronoun	Sentence
I	**I** am sick today.
you	**You** are a student.
he/she	**She** plays soccer.
it	**It** is large.
we	**We** read the news.
you	**You** are students.
they	**They** are busy.

Contractions

I am = **I'm**
you are = **you're**
he is = **he's**
she is = **she's**
it is = **it's**
we are = **we're**
they are = **they're**

Object Pronouns (p. 70)

Object pronouns take the place of object nouns. They show to whom something happened or who got something. They come after a verb or preposition.

Object Pronoun	Sentence
me	Please help **me** understand.
you	Fatima works with **you**.
him/her	A woman is talking to **him**.
it	People are next to **it**.
us	They live next door to **us**.
you	The teacher will give information to **you**.
them	The mother is watching **them**.

A **verb** is an action word.   Example: He **works** in a big office.

Simple Present Tense (pp. 5, 17, 30, 68, 121)

Use the **simple present tense** to tell about an action that is true now or that generally happens.

Simple Present Tense with *be*	
Affirmative	**Negative**
I **am** from China.	I **am not** from Japan.
You **are** young.	You **are not** old.
Francisco **is** a student.	She **is not** a student.
My mother and I **are** at home.	We **are not** at school.
Tom and Tim **are** in Los Angeles.	They **are not** in New York City.

Contractions

I am = **I'm**

you are = **you're**

he is = **he's**

she is = **she's**

it is = **it's**

we are = **we're**

they are = **they're**

is not = **isn't**

are not = **aren't**

Simple Present Tense with *have*			
Affirmative		**Negative**	
I You We They	**have** a small apartment.	I You We They	**do not have** a large home.
He She It	**has** a clean bedroom.	He She It	**does not have** a messy room.

Contractions

does not = **doesn't**

do not = **don't**

Simple Present Tense with Regular Verbs			
Affirmative		**Negative**	
I You We They	**work** on Saturdays.	I You We They	**do not work** on Sundays.
He She It	**works** every day.	He She It	**does not work** every day.

Rule

Add an **s** to a verb for **he**, **she**, and **it**.

Present Continuous Tense (pp. 69, 82)

The **present continuous tense** tells about an action happening right now.

Use **be** and a main verb. Add **ing** to the end of the verb.

Present Continuous Tense	
Affirmative	**Negative**
I **am eating** right now.	I **am not eating** right now.
You **are reading** right now.	You **are not reading** right now.
He **is writing** right now.	He **is not writing** right now.
We **are dancing** right now.	We **are not dancing** right now.
They **are running** right now.	They **are not running** right now.

Simple Past Tense (pp. 83, 84, 109, 110, 121)

Use the **simple past tense** of a verb to tell about an action that happened in the past.

Simple Past Tense with *be*	
Affirmative	Negative
I **was** at the game.	I **was** **not** at the mall.
You **were** hungry before lunch.	You **were** **not** hungry after lunch.
Francisco **was** tired on Sunday night.	He **was** **not** tired on Saturday night.
We **were** on a bus yesterday.	We **were** **not** on a plane yesterday.
You **were** my classmates last year.	You **were** **not** my neighbors last year.
They **were** busy on Saturday morning.	They **were** **not** busy on Saturday night.

Contractions

was not = **wasn't**

were not = **weren't**

Simple Past Tense with Regular Verbs	
Affirmative	Negative
Francisco **helped** Maria.	Maria **did not help** her mother.
I **lived** in Haiti last year.	I **did not live** in Houston last year.
They **studied** on Sunday afternoon.	They **did not study** on Saturday night.
The Garcia family **shopped** for food.	The Garcia family **did not shop** for clothes.

Contractions

did not = **didn't**

Rules for Simple Past Tense		
If . . .	Then . . .	Example
If the verb ends in a **consonant**	then add **ed**.	help → help**ed**
If the verb ends in **e**	then add **d**.	live → live**d**
If the verb ends in **consonant + y**	then change **y** to **i** and add **ed**.	study → stud**ied**
If the verb ends in **vowel + consonant**	then double the consonant and add **ed**.	shop → shop**ped**

Past Tense of Irregular Verbs

Base Form	Simple Past Tense	Base Form	Simple Past Tense	Base Form	Simple Past Tense
be	was/were	forget	forgot	ride	rode
become	became	get	got	ring	rang
begin	began	give	gave	run	ran
break	broke	go	went	say	said
bring	brought	grow	grew	see	saw
buy	bought	have	had	sell	sold
catch	caught	hear	heard	send	sent
choose	chose	hold	held	sing	sang
come	came	hurt	hurt	sit	sat
cost	cost	keep	kept	sleep	slept
cut	cut	know	knew	speak	spoke
do	did	leave	left	spend	spent
drink	drank	let	let	stand	stood
drive	drove	light	lit	take	took
eat	ate	lose	lost	teach	taught
fall	fell	make	made	tell	told
feel	felt	meet	met	think	thought
fight	fought	pay	paid	wear	wore
find	found	put	put	win	won
fly	flew	read	read	write	wrote

Future Tense (pp. 95, 96, 121)

The **future tense** describes events that happen after the present.

For actions in the future, use **be** + **going to** + verb.

Future Tense with *be going to*

Affirmative	Negative
I **am going to go** shopping tonight.	I **am not going to go** shopping tomorrow.
You **are going to buy** food tomorrow.	You **are not going to buy** food tonight.
The trip **is going to be** great.	The trip **isn't going to be** boring.
We **are going to read** four books.	We **are not going to read** magazines.
You **are going to have** a test next week.	You **are not going to have** a test tomorrow.
Students **are going to have** a picnic.	They **aren't going to have** a parade.

There is / There are (p. 57)

Statements with *There is / There are*		
	Affirmative	**Negative**
Singular	**There is** a mall next to the park.	**There is no** mall across from the park. **There is not** a mall across from the park.
Plural	**There are** stores in the mall.	**There are no** stores in the park. **There are not any** stores in the park.
Noncount Nouns	**There is** grass in the park.	**There is no** grass in the mall. **There is not any** grass in the mall.

Contractions

there is = **there's**

is not = **isn't**

are not = **aren't**

there is not = **there's not** = there isn't

Imperative Form (p. 31)

Use the imperative form to give instructions, directions, or orders.

The imperative is like the simple present tense verb for **you** without a subject.

Simple Present	Imperative Sentences	
	Affirmative	**Negative**
You write a story.	**Write** a story.	**Do not write** a story.
You get six onions.	**Get** six onions.	**Do not get** six onions.
You go to the market.	**Go** to the market.	**Do not go** to the market.

Contractions

do not = **don't**

Modal Verbs

Should (p. 58)

Use should to make suggestions.

Should goes before a verb.

Should for Suggestions	
Affirmative	**Negative**
You **should visit** Francisco's neighborhood.	You **should not miss** it.
Francisco **should be** quiet in the bookstore.	He **should not talk** to Maria.
People **should** wear a hat in the sun.	Students **should not** wear a hat in class.

Contractions

should not = **shouldn't**

Want and *Would Like* (p. 96)

Want and would like tell about a wish, request, or invitation.

Want is informal. Would like is formal.

Informal (want)	Formal (would like)
Francisco **wants to go** to the park.	He **would like to go** to the park.
I **want to be** a waitress.	I **would like to be** a waitress.
I **want** you **to come** to lunch.	I **would like** you **to come** to lunch.
We **want** you **to be** on time.	We **would like** you **to be** on time.

SENTENCES

Complete Sentences (p. 19)

A **sentence** is a group of words. The words express a complete thought.

A **complete sentence** has a subject and a verb.

The **subject** tells who or what the sentence is about.

The **verb** tells about the subject.

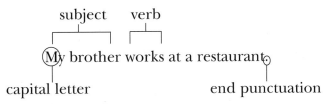

Incomplete Sentences (incorrect)	Complete Sentences (correct)
Carlos volleyball team. (no verb)	Carlos is on the volleyball team.
Writes in her journal. (no subject)	Hong writes in her journal.

Subject-Verb Agreement (p. 122)

The **subject** and **verb** in a sentence must **agree** in number.

When a subject is singular, the verb must be singular.

When a subject is plural, the verb must be plural.

Subject-Verb Agreement	
singular subject + singular verb	**plural subject + plural verb**
She is a doctor.	**They are** teachers.
The man cooks breakfast every day.	**The children play** in the park.

ADJECTIVES (p. 4, 16, 56, 83)

Adjectives describe or give information about people, places, or things.

Adjectives go after the verb **be** or before a noun.

Add a comma (,) or the word **and** between adjectives.

I am **smart**.	The air is **fresh** and **clean**.
Mrs. Moore is a **good** teacher.	The **tall** woman runs every day.
Her classroom is **big**.	There is a **huge**, **beautiful** park.

Quantity Adjectives (p. 58)

Quantity adjectives answer the questions how much or how many.

Quantity Adjectives	
Large Amounts	**Small Amounts**
There are **many** trees in the park.	There are **some** vegetables.
There are **a lot of** children.	There are **a few** restaurants.
There are **nineteen** magazines.	I had **a little** tea.

Possessive Adjectives (p. 18)

Possessive adjectives tell who owns something.

They go before nouns.

Possessive Adjective	Examples
my	I am a student. **My** name is Rafael.
your	You are a freshman. **Your** homeroom is Room 21.
his	Sam is a student. **His** teacher is Mr. Li.
her	This is Julia. This is **her** classroom.
its	The computer is in the office. **Its** screen is on.
our	We are studying biology. **Our** teacher is Mrs. Johnson.
your	You are good students. **Your** grades are excellent.
their	Mr. and Mrs. Garcia are parents. **Their** son is Francisco.

Comparative and Superlative Adjectives (p. 94)

Comparative adjectives compare two things.

Add **than** after the comparative form.

> Maria is **younger than** Francisco.
>
> Maria's costume is **more interesting than** Tara's costume.

Forms of Comparative Adjectives		
If . . .	Then . . .	Example
If the adjective has one syllable	then add **er**.	small → small**er**
If the adjective has two syllables and ends in **y**	then change the **y** to **i** and add **er**.	happy → happ**ier**
If the adjective ends in **e**	then add **r**.	nice → nice**r**
If the adjective has two or more syllables	then add **more** before the adjective.	interesting → **more** interesting
If the adjective is irregular	then use the comparative adjective form.	good → **better** bad → **worse**

Superlative adjectives compare more than two things.

Add **the** before the superlative form.

> Maria is **the youngest** person in her family.
>
> Maria's costume is **the most interesting** in her class.

Forms of Superlative Adjectives		
If . . .	Then . . .	Example
The adjective has one syllable	then add **est**.	small → small**est**
The adjective has two syllables and ends in **y**	then change the **y** to **i** and add **est**.	happy → happ**iest**
The adjective ends in **e**	then add **st**.	nice → nice**st**
The adjective has two or more syllables	then add **most** before the adjective.	interesting → **most** interesting
The adjective is irregular	then use the superlative adjective form.	good → **best** bad → **worst**

ADVERBS (p. 70)

Adverbs answer the questions *how, when*, or *where*.

They give details about verbs, adjectives, and other adverbs.

To make many adverbs, add **ly** to the adjective form.

Really, yesterday, and *very* are also adverbs.

Adverbs	
Use	**Purpose**
She watches them **carefully**.	The adverb tells **how** she **watches** them.
It is **really** hot.	The adverb tells **how hot** it is.
Yesterday, I ran.	The adverb tells **when I ran.**
The beach is **nearby**.	The adverb tells **where** the beach **is.**

Adverbs of Frequency (p. 44)

Adverbs of frequency answer the question *how often*.

Adverbs of Frequency		
How often?	**Adverb of Frequency**	**Example**
100% of the time	always	I walk to school every day. I **always** walk to school.
	usually	I bring my lunch four days per week. I **usually** bring my lunch.
	often	I arrive early three days per week. I **often** arrive early.
	sometimes	I am very tired one or two days per week. I am **sometimes** very tired.
0% of the time	never	I don't dance. I **never** dance.

PREPOSITIONS (pp. 18, 44, 68, 82)

Prepositions tell where, when, and how something happens.

They usually have a noun after them.

preposition + noun = prepositional phrase

Examples:

New Year's Eve is **on December 31**.

Cinco de Mayo is very popular **in the U.S**.

Francisco celebrates his birthday **at home**.

The Garcia family goes **to the** *Cinco de Mayo* **parade**.

Common Prepositions				
about above across around at	before behind below beside between	by during except for from	in into of on over	through to under with without

Prepositions of Time and Location

Time expressions tell when something happens or how long something lasts.

Example: I play baseball **for** two hours **in** the afternoon.

Location phrases tell where something is located.

Example: The bedroom is **next to** the kitchen.

When?	**in** the morning	**on** Saturday	**at** 12:00 p.m./**at** noon
How long?	**for** two hours	**for** one week	**from** 3:00 **to** 5:00
Where?	**on** Elm Street	**at** Oak Street Park	**across from** Room 21

QUESTIONS AND ANSWERS (p. 43, 110)

There are two kinds of questions: yes/no questions and wh- questions.

The answer to a *yes/no* question is either **yes** or **no**.

Yes/No Questions with *be*			
Verb Tense	Statement	*Yes/No* Question	Short Answer
simple present	The kitchen **is** big.	**Is** the kitchen big?	Yes, it **is**. No, it **is not**.
	The rooms **are** small.	**Are** the rooms small?	Yes, they **are**. No, they **are not**.
present continuous	She **is being** funny.	**Is** she **being** funny?	Yes, she **is**. No, she **is not**.
simple past	The window **was** open.	**Was** the window open?	Yes, it **was**. No, it **was not**.
	The doors **were** closed.	**Were** the doors closed?	Yes, they **were**. No, they **were not**.
future	You **are going to be** here tomorrow.	**Are** you **going to be** here tomorrow?	Yes, I **am**. No, I **am not**.
	They **are going to be** busy this weekend.	**Are** they **going to be** busy this weekend?	Yes, they **are**. No, they **are not**.

Contractions

was not = **wasn't**

were not = **weren't**

we are = **we're**

they are = **they're**

Yes/No Questions with Other Verbs

Verb Tense	Statement	Yes/No Question	Short Answer
simple present	She **likes** the house.	**Does** she **like** the house?	Yes, she **does**. No, she **does not**.
	They **study** in the kitchen.	**Do** they **study** in the kitchen?	Yes, they **do**. No, they **do not**.
present continuous	You **are learning** math.	**Are** you **learning** math?	Yes, we **are**. No, we **are not**.
simple past	You **ate** in the kitchen.	**Did** you **eat** in the kitchen?	Yes, I **did**. No, I **did not**.
future	He **is going to clean** on Friday.	**Is** he **going to clean** on Friday?	Yes, he **is**. No, he **isn't**.

Contractions

does not = **doesn't**

do not = **don't**

did not = **didn't**

Wh- Questions

Verb Tense	Wh- Question	Answer
simple present	**What** is Mr. Garcia's favorite holiday?	Mr. Garcia's favorite holiday is *Cinco de Mayo*.
present continuous	**How** is the Garcia family celebrating Maria's birthday?	The Garcia family is having a picnic to celebrate Maria's birthday.
simple past	**When** was the Oak Street School Festival?	The Oak Street School Festival was last week.
	Who went to the movies with you?	Yoko went to the movies with me.
future	**Why** is Maria going to stay home?	Maria is going to stay home because she is sick.
	Where are you going to work?	I am going to work at Ming's Chinese Restaurant.

PUNCTUATION

Period (.)
end of a statement   I go to school.
after an abbreviation   Ave.   Mr.   St.   Dr.

Question Mark (?)
end of a question   How are you?

Exclamation Point (!)
after a strong sentence   My room is very small!

Apostrophe (')
to show possession   The girl's book is on the desk.
in a contraction   he's   it's   isn't   weren't   didn't

Comma (,)
to separate things in a list   Victoria, Yang, and I are classmates.
to separate adjectives   The short, funny man is in the park.
between the day and year in a date   July 4, 1776
between city and state   Dallas, Texas
after the opening of a friendly letter   Dear Roxana,
after the closing of a letter   Sincerely,

CAPITALIZATION

Capitalize the first word in a sentence.   He is from Los Angeles.
Capitalize the pronoun **I**.   Jose and **I** are best friends.
Capitalize proper nouns.

    people   **G**eorge **W**ashington
    places   **P**uebla, **M**exico
    days   **M**onday
    months   **F**ebruary
    holidays   **T**hanksgiving
    special events   **O**lympics
    nationalities   **B**ritish
    languages   **S**panish
    schools   **W**est **H**igh **S**chool
    abbreviations   **D**r.   **R**d.
    titles   *Step-by-Step Writing*

COMMONLY MISSPELLED WORDS

Word	Definition	Sentence
allowed aloud	permitted; with permission out loud, spoken	Being late is not **allowed.** The student read her poem **aloud** in class.
among between	included within in the space separating two things	**Among** her many friends, she is happy. The cat was **between** the wall and the car.
board bored	a classroom object for writing on tired, uninterested	Please write the answer on the **board.** The class is not interesting, so I am **bored.**
buy by	to pay for something next to	I **buy** a newspaper every morning. The chair is **by** the door.
cite sight site	to give credit to a source of information the sense of seeing a real location or one on Internet	In his report, the student **cites** several books. My **sight** is good. I don't need glasses. The information is on our Web **site.**
desert dessert	dry land of sand and rock, with little rain food after a meal, like cake or fruit	The Sahara **Desert** is in Africa. We had apple pie and coffee for **dessert.**
for four	with the purpose of the number 4	I am buying tomatoes **for** the salad. The boy has **four** sisters.
hear here	to receive sound with the ears at or in this place	I **hear** the sound of a police car. We have lived **here** for ten years.
it's its	a contraction of *it is* the possessive form of *it*	**It's** raining today, but it wasn't yesterday. The house has a tree by **its** door.
than then	used to show comparison the next in an order of events	The weather is hotter **than** it was last year. I went to school and **then** I went to work.
their there they're	the possessive form of *they* at or to a specific place used to begin a statement a contraction of *they are*	**Their** apartment is on the second floor. We went **there** after school. **There** are twenty students in class today. **They're** tired because they ran home.
to too two	toward, in the direction of in addition, as well, also the number 2	She goes **to** Vietnam every year. The book was good. The movie was good **too.** People have **two** legs.
we're were where	a contraction of *we are* past tense of *be* in or at which place, a certain location	**We're** having dinner after work. They **were** at the store this morning. **Where** are you from?
who's whose	a contraction of *who is* the possessive form of *who*	**Who's** going to come to our party? **Whose** coat is this?
your you're	the possessive form of *you* a contraction of *you are*	Is this **your** hat? **You're** sick. You should stay home.

Paragraph Model

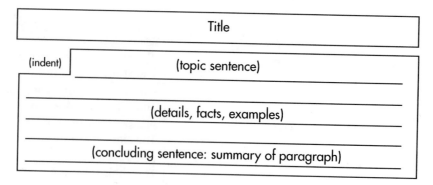

Friendly Letter Model   Formal Letter Model

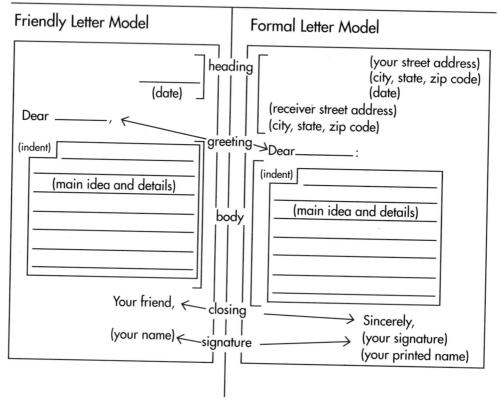

CITATION GUIDE

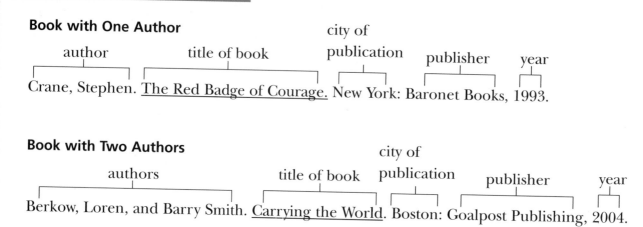

Book with One Author

	author	title of book	city of publication	publisher	year

Crane, Stephen. The Red Badge of Courage. New York: Baronet Books, 1993.

Book with Two Authors

Berkow, Loren, and Barry Smith. Carrying the World. Boston: Goalpost Publishing, 2004.

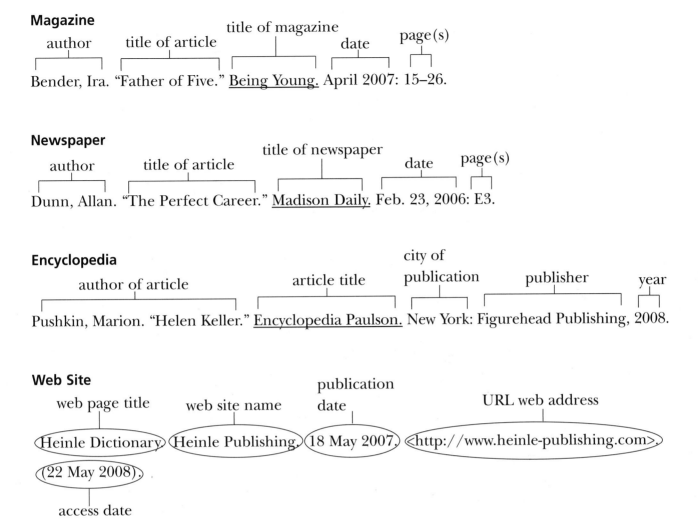

Magazine

author   title of article   title of magazine   date   page(s)

Bender, Ira. "Father of Five." <u>Being Young.</u> April 2007: 15–26.

Newspaper

author   title of article   title of newspaper   date   page(s)

Dunn, Allan. "The Perfect Career." <u>Madison Daily.</u> Feb. 23, 2006: E3.

Encyclopedia

author of article   article title   city of publication   publisher   year

Pushkin, Marion. "Helen Keller." <u>Encyclopedia Paulson.</u> New York: Figurehead Publishing, 2008.

Web Site

web page title   web site name   publication date   URL web address

Heinle Dictionary. Heinle Publishing. 18 May 2007. <http://www.heinle-publishing.com>.

22 May 2008.

access date

STUDENT WRITING RUBRIC

Look at the writing. Read the sentences below. Add your own criteria at the end of the list. Do you agree with the sentences? Look at the score chart. Then, write a score next to each sentence. Add comments.

Score			Meaning
5			I strongly agree.
4			I agree.
3			I have no opinion.
2			I disagree.
1			I strongly disagree.

Criteria	Score	Comments
1. Development of Ideas		
The author answered the prompt completely.		
The writing has a purpose or main idea.		
All the ideas connect to a main idea.		
The details support the main ideas.		
The author shows an understanding of the topic.		
2. Organization		
The writing has an introduction, a body, and a conclusion.		
The ideas are in a logical order.		
The paragraphs are well-organized.		
3. Voice		
The author's voice is original.		
The writing is interesting.		
The writing addresses the correct audience.		
4. Fluency and Focus		
The writing maintains focus.		
There are meaningful transitions between ideas.		
The sentences and paragraphs are clear and concise.		
There are different sentence types.		
5. Conventions		
The sentences use correct grammar.		
The words and phrases are specific and meaningful.		
The punctuation and capitalization are correct.		
The spelling is correct.		
The author cites sources correctly.		
6. Presentation		
The presentation is in the correct format.		
The author included a title, name, and date.		
The first line of every paragraph is indented.		
7. My Criteria		
-		
-		
Total		
	÷ 25	
Grade (out of 5)		

What your grade means:

5	4	3	2	1
excellent	great	good	need more practice	incomplete

GLOSSARY

abbreviations, p. 85 Abbreviations are short forms of words. For example, the abbreviation of the word Street is St.

action, p. 71, 72, 111, 112 The action is what is happening.

action verb, p. 17 An action verb tells what someone or something does.

address, p. 85 An address gives the name and location of the receiver of a letter.

adjective, p. 4, 16 An adjective describes a noun or a pronoun.

adverb, p. 44, 70 An adverb describes verbs or adjectives. Many adverbs end in –ly.

antonym, p. 108 An antonym is a word that has an opposite meaning to another word.

article, p. 4 The article (*a, an,* or *the*) is before a noun.

audience, p. 45, 97 The audience is a person who reads your work.

beginning, p. 111, 112 The beginning of a story introduces the story and tells about the setting and the characters.

body, p. 85 The body is the message of a letter.

capitalize, p. 7, 43 To capitalize is to make small letters larger. Example: b → B

categorize, p. 7 To categorize is to group similar ideas together by topic.

characters, p. 71, 72, 111, 112 Characters are the people in a story.

chronological order, p. 97 Chronological order is the order in which events really happen in a story.

cite, p. 24, 123 To cite is to tell where a writer got his or her information.

click, p. 12 To click is to choose an online option with the mouse.

closing, p. 85 In the closing, the sender of a letter says "good-bye" to the receiver of the letter.

comparative adjectives, p. 94 Comparative adjectives compare two people, places, or things.

concluding sentence, p. 112 The concluding sentence ends the story and tells what it means.

connecting words, p. 45 A connecting word, like *or, but, and* or *because,* joins ideas or sentences.

contraction, p. 5, 6, 17, 57 A contraction, like *he's* and *can't,* is one word made from two words put together with an apostrophe.

copy, p. 76 On a computer, to copy text is the first step to transfer text from one place to another. To copy, use Ctrl+C or Command+C.

count noun, p. 32 A count noun is a noun that you can count. It has both singular and plural forms.

description, p. 72 A description is the details of a person, place, thing, or event.

descriptive adjectives, p. 68 Descriptive adjectives give details to help the reader visualize what a person, place, or thing is like.

descriptive writing, p. 20, 72 Descriptive writing gives details and information about a topic.

details, p. 59 Details give more information about a main idea.

dictionary, p. 71 A dictionary is a list of words with their meanings.

download, p. 64 To download is to get files from the Internet onto your computer.

draft, p. 11, 23, 37, 49, 63, 75, 89, 101, 115, 127 A draft, like a first draft, third draft, or final draft, is one version of writing. To draft, along with to revise, is step three of the writing process.

edit, p. 12, 24, 38, 50, 64, 76, 90, 102, 116, 128 To edit is to make writing better by making small changes. Editing is step four of the writing process.

e-mail, p. 86 An e-mail is an electronic message sent using the Internet.

end, p. 111, 112 The end of a story tells what the story means or why it is important.

end punctuation, p. 33 End punctuation, like a period, is the mark at the end of a sentence to make written ideas clear.

exact phrase, p. 38 An exact phrase is used to find what you are looking for on the Internet. Quotation marks are used around the exact phrase to narrow your search.

expository writing, p. 46 Expository writing explains, describes, or gives information to an audience.

exclamation point, p. 33 An exclamation point is a punctuation mark used at the end of a sentence to make a statement stronger. It looks like this: !

first person, p. 112 In a first person narrative, the writer uses a person in the story to tell the story, using the pronouns *I, me, we,* and *us.*

form, p. 97 Form is the shape or style of something.

formal letter, p. 98 A formal letter gives more background information and uses more formal language than friendly letters. A formal letter is usually used when a writer is writing to someone they don't know. Business letters and event invitations are examples of formal letters.

friendly letter, p. 86, 98 A friendly letter is an informal letter that is written to a friend or family member.

future tense, p. 95 The future tense of a verb tells about an action that will happen later, or in the future.

general information, p. 71 General information gives information about a topic, like time and place.

greeting, p. 85 In the greeting of a letter, the writer says "hello" to the receiver.

heading, p. 85 The heading gives the date of a letter.

highlight, p. 76 To highlight is to select a word or words by holding down the left button on a mouse, running the arrow over the word or words, and then releasing the button.

hits, p. 38 Hits are the Web sites you find in a search on the Internet.

hyperlink, p. 12, 24, 38, 90, 102 A hyperlink is something you can click on a Web page, opening a new Web site.

imperative form, p. 31 Imperative form gives a command or instructions.

indent, p. 59 When you indent, you leave space before writing a line of text.

informal message, p. 86 An informal message, like a friendly letter or an e-mail, is usually written to a friend or family member. It often tells how the author is feeling and about recent events or activities.

informational writing, p. 8 Informational writing gives information about a topic. Information forms, surveys, and reports are examples of informational writing.

Internet, p. 12 The Internet is a world-wide computer network.

journal, p. 72 A journal, or diary, is a book or Web site where you write about your experiences.

keyword, p. 12, 76 An keyword is used to search a topic on the Internet.

location phrases, p. 68 A location phrase tells where something is located.

main idea, p. 59 The main idea (or controlling idea) is the focus, central thought, or purpose of a paragraph.

middle, p. 111, 112 The middle of a story gives details about the action or plot.

narrative description, p. 20 A narrative description describes a part of your life, like your home or family.

narrow, p. 38 To narrow is to reduce or limit your Internet search.

noncount noun, p. 32 A noncount noun is a noun that you cannot count. It does not have a plural form.

noun, p. 4 A noun is a person, place, or thing.

open, p. 76 On a computer, to open a document or file means to make it appear on the screen for use.

order of importance, p. 45 Order of importance gives central ideas first, and then less important ideas.

ordinal numbers, p. 42 Ordinal numbers show the order or sequence in which something happens. Example: first, second, or last.

organize, p. 10, 22, 36, 48, 62, 74, 88, 100, 114, 126 To organize is to put something in order. To organize is step two of the writing process.

paragraph, p. 59 A paragraph is a group of sentences about a topic.

paraphrase, p. 123 To paraphrase is to retell in a writer's own words information from a source.

paste, p. 76 On the computer, to paste text is the second step to transfer text from one place to another. To paste, use Ctrl+V or Command+V.

period, p. 33 A period is a punctuation mark that is a dot at the end of a sentence. It looks like this: .

persuasive writing, p. 60 In persuasive writing, the author tries to make an audience agree with the writer's opinion.

personal narrative, p. 112 A personal narrative tells a story from the author's point of view.

plot, p. 111 The plot is the series of main events that make up a story.

plural form, p. 16 The plural form of a noun tells about more than one person, place, or thing.

point of view, p. 112 A point of view is the way the narrator looks at or understands something.

possessive adjective, p. 18 A possessive adjective is the possessive form of a personal pronoun, such as *my, your, his, her, their,* or *our.*

possessive noun, p. 18 A possessive noun is the name of an owner. Posessive nouns include an apostrophe. Example: Francisco's book

preposition, p. 18 A preposition is a short connecting word, such as *to, from, with,* and *in,* that shows how two things or ideas are related.

prepositional phrases, p. 44 A prepositional phrase starts with a preposition and ends with a noun or pronoun. Prepositional phrases are used to show location, time, or description.

present continuous tense, p. 69 The present continuous tense tells what is happening right now.

pre-write, p. 10, 22, 36, 48, 62, 74, 88, 100, 114, 126 To pre-write is to take notes about what you are going to write about. Pre-writing is the first step of the writing process.

print, p. 64 To print from a computer is to put words or images onto paper.

pronoun, p. 70 A pronoun a word that takes place of a noun, like *he, she, it, we,* or *they.*

publish, p. 12, 24, 38, 50, 64, 76, 90, 102, 116, 128 To publish a piece of writing, the final draft is hand-written or typed on the computer for an audience to read. To publish is the last step of the writing process.

purpose, p. 97 The purpose is why the writer is writing.

quantity adjectives, p. 58 Quantity adjectives are adjectives that tell the amount, or how many, of a noun there is. Example: *Many* books; *some* students.

question mark, p. 33 A question mark is a punctuation mark at the end of a sentence to show that the sentence asks a question. It looks like this: ?

receiver, p. 85, 86 The receiver is the person who a letter is written for.

return address, p. 85 A return address gives the name and location of the writer of a letter.

results bar, p. 38 The results bar shows the information that is searched for on the Internet. It is located at the top of the Web page.

revise, p. 11, 23, 37, 49, 63, 75, 89, 101, 115, 127 To revise is to make changes to your draft of writing to improve it. To revise, along with to draft, is step three of the writing process.

search, p. 12, 24 To search is to look up information on the Internet.

search engine, p. 12 A search engine is used to look up information on the Internet.

sensory adjectives, p. 56 Sensory adjectives describe how things smell, feel, taste, sound, and look.

sentence, p. 19 A sentence is a group of words that contains a subject and a verb and expresses a complete thought.

sequential order, p. 33 Sequential order tells the order of events.

sequence words, p. 33 Sequence words are used to show the order of events.

setting, p. 71, 72, 111, 112 Setting is the time and place of the story.

should or shouldn't, p. 58 Should or shouldn't are verbs used to make suggestions.

signal words, p. 45 Signal words, like *too* and *as well,* add information in a story.

signature, p. 85 The signature is the signed name under the closing in a letter.

simple past tense, p. 8, 109 The simple past tense describes events or actions completed in the past.

simple present tense, p. 17 The simple present tense describes things that are generally true or happen regularly.

simple verb tense, p. 121 Simple verb tense is a verb with no endings or other changes. For example, *walk, speak,* and *see* are in the simple verb tense.

singular form, p. 16 The singular form of a noun names one person, place, or thing.

source, p. 24, 123 A source is the place where the writer got the information used in his or her writing.

spatial order, p. 19 Spatial order gives information by location, or space.

specific details, p. 71 Specific details give more exact information about a subject.

statement with *be,* p. 5 A statement with *be* is a sentence using a form of the verb *to be.* Example: Francisco is a student.

statement with *There is/ There are,* p. 57 A statement with *there is/there are* is a sentence using the simple present tense of the verb *to be. There is* is used with singular nouns and noncount nouns. *There are* is used with plural nouns.

stories, p. 72 Stories are pieces of writing that are made up in the writer's mind.

subject, p. 19 The subject tells who or what the sentence is about.

subject pronoun, p. 6 A subject pronoun is used in place of a noun that is the subject of a sentence.

subject-verb agreement, p. 122 The subject-verb agreement rule states that the subject and verb in a sentence must agree in number.

summary, p. 124 A summary gives the facts and main ideas from a longer passage or story.

summary paragraph, p. 123 A summary paragraph tells the main ideas and the important details from a longer passage

superlative adjectives, p. 94 Superlative adjectives compare three or more people, places, or things.

supporting sentence, p. 59, 60, 112 A supporting sentence gives details or more information about the topic.

synonyms, p. 56,108 Synonym is a word that has the same or similar meaning to another word.

technical writing, p. 34 Technical writing often gives instructions. It sometimes explains how to do a procedure.

time expressions, p. 82 Time expressions tell when something happens or how long something lasts.

timeline, p. 97 A timeline organizes events by time.

topic, p. 7, 45, 59, 97 A topic is what the paragraph or story is about.

topic sentence, p. 59, 60, 112, 123 A topic sentence is the sentence that gives the main idea of the paragraph.

thesaurus, p. 56 A thesaurus groups words together into synonyms and antonyms.

verb, p. 17, 19 The verb tells the action of the subject.

wh- questions, p. 43, 110 *Wh-* questions, like *who, what, when, where,* and *how,* are questions that ask for information.

transition words, p. 111 Transition words connect sentences and ideas.

INDEX